UNWIN HYMAN SHORT STORIES

SCHOOL'S OK

INCLUDING
FOLLOW ON
ACTIVITIES

EDITED BY JOSIE KARAVASIL

AND ROY BLATCHFORD

Published by
UNWIN HYMAN LIMITED
15/17 Broadwick Street
London W1V 1FP

This selection © Josie Karavasil 1982
Introduction and notes © Roy Blatchford 1985
The copyright of each story remains the
property of the author.

First published in 1982 by Evans Brothers
Published by Bell & Hyman Limited 1985
Reprinted 1986, 1987
Reprinted by Unwin Hyman Limited 1988

British Library Cataloguing in Publication Data
School's O.K.—2nd ed.—(Unwin Hyman
   short stories)
   1. Children's stories, English   2. Students—
  Juvenile fiction
   I. Karavasil, Josie   II. Blatchford, Roy
   823'.01'08354J   PZ5
ISBN 0 7135 2450–2

Printed and bound in Great Britain by
Billing & Sons Ltd. Worcester

Series cover design by Iain Lanyon
Cover illustration details from 'Kids' by Martin Handford

UNWIN HYMAN
Short Stories
Collections
Plays

Series editor: Roy Blatchford
Advisers: Jane Leggett and Gervase Phinn

Unwin Hyman Short Stories
Openings   edited by Roy Blatchford
Round Two   edited by Roy Blatchford
School's OK   edited by Josie Karavasil and Roy Blatchford
Stepping Out   edited by Jane Leggett
That'll Be The Day   edited by Roy Blatchford
Sweet and Sour   edited by Gervase Phinn
It's Now or Never   edited by Jane Leggett and Roy Blatchford
Pigs is Pigs   edited by Trevor Millum
Dreams and Resolutions   edited by Roy Blatchford

Unwin Hyman Collections
Free As I Know   edited by Beverley Naidoo
Solid Ground   edited by Jane Leggett and Sue Libovitch
In Our Image   edited by Andrew Goodwyn

Unwin Hyman Plays
Stage Write   edited by Gervase Phinn

CONTENTS

INTRODUCTION

School and schooldays have always been popular topics with writers – probably because it is a subject which always stirs vivid memories and about which everyone feels they know something. From *Tom Brown's Schooldays*, the *Just William* stories and *Greyfriars* to *Grange Hill* today the tradition has been rich and varied – and one that, with the growth of comprehensive schools in real life, has undergone interesting and significant change! These ten stories have been written specially for *School's O.K.* by some of the best of our contemporary authors. They centre around school life set in the past, present and future, and they explore with humour and realism the major themes of school life: pupils' attitudes to each other, relationships with teachers, classroom excitement and tensions.

The stories are not set in any particular order. There is no need therefore to move chronologically through the collection, but an idea encountered in one story can certainly be linked with another. For example, 'Flying Dustbins' and 'The Rescue of Karen Arscott' focus on the perennial problem of playground bullies. 'A Day Too Late' and 'The

Woodwork Class' are sensitively cast accounts of racial prejudice, while 'Woof' is a powerful tale of tensions between one pupil and his teachers which have literally explosive consequences.

In contrast, 'Do You Read Me?' and 'School Play' are marvellously funny snapshots of school 'characters'. A more unusual theme – that of children in search of their cultural identity through language – is cleverly explored in 'Suddenly There Came a Crack in the Ice'. Perhaps the most intriguing in the collection, and one which repays repeated readings, is 'The Sleeping Beauty of Anton P'ntarr', which skilfully mixes the science-fiction and love story genres and ends with a splendid twist. The final story 'Sea-Coal' is both compelling and provocative in its presentation of today's young school-leaver alongside his counterpart fifty years ago.

Each story is followed by a brief comment by the author. The *Follow On* section contains material to help pupils discuss and appreciate the short story genre, together with various discussion, writing and drama ideas to take readers into and beyond each of the ten stories.

School's O.K. is a strong and engaging collection of school stories which will have a broad appeal across the lower and middle secondary age range.

R.B.

DO YOU READ ME?
Jan Mark

It was the custom to bring back yearly reports, signed, at the beginning of the autumn term, to prove that they had been shown to parents, or at least to a competent forger. Fenton, the Fifth Year tutor, was At Home in his office on Friday morning to receive them. When Rodney King clinked in with his report and laid it on the desk under Fenton's nose, Fenton looked at it, looked at Rodney, crossed his knees, folded his hands, and sat back with the air of a man who has prepared a little speech.

"It's a good one, in most respects, especially for Art and Design, I see. A+, eh? Parents pleased?"

Rodney nodded.

"Only there's this nasty little rider here, to the effect that you have difficulty in communicating. What does that mean, do you think?"

Rodney shrugged.

"It could mean that you don't say much for yourself. Might that be the trouble? A bit of a loner, are you? No close friends?"

Rodney made a non-committal noise through the

7

slit between his front teeth.

"Your written work's excellent – no complaints from anyone about that – but you've got to learn to verbalize. You'll be doing CSE English, this year. What's going to happen when you come to the oral?"

Rodney's hand described a gesture that dealt dismissively with the English oral. He took a step backward to indicate that he thought the interview might usefully be concluded.

"It's no good relying on badges to do your communicating for you," Fenton said. "I mean, it's very reassuring to see you covered in slogans for Nuclear Disarmament and Rock against Racism, but any idiot can pin on a badge. How many have you got?

Rodney was moved to verbalize. "Seventy-three."

"And are you wearing them all?"

"Yes, Sir."

"Look, King, don't feel that I'm criticizing gratuitously, but when the Headmaster abolished school uniform for the Fifth and Sixth Forms, I doubt if he intended you to come to school in armour plate. You look like a pearly king under a microscope. The people who sit behind you don't do any work; they spend all their time reading your badges."

"I could move to the back," Rodney offered, helpfully.

"Don't think of it," Fenton said. "We might lose touch with you altogether. Just move the badges from the rear of that cut-price Biggles outfit – and the sleeves. Be selective, King. Use your designer's eye. Just a few, here and there, tastefully arranged, should be quite aesthetically pleasing. We'll get the message – *one* message at a time. OK?"

Rodney returned to school on Monday with his bomber jacket feeling several pounds lighter, and ran into Fenton in the corridor where he was pinning a sheet of foolscap to the Fifth Year notice board.

"Book Fair," said Fenton. "October 8th, St Stephen's Hall. Want to come? Sign here."

Rodney wove a deprecating pattern with his toes on the vinyl tiles, and the collar of his jacket rose about his ears.

"Oh, King, what eloquent shoulders you do have," Fenton said. "I'll take silence for consent. There, you can put your name down right at the top of the list. I suppose that elaborate routine is meant to suggest that you have nothing to write with? Tough titty," said Fenton, whipping out his biro, and writing Rodney's name in cock-eyed capitals at the head of the paper. "No one," Fenton observed, "would know that you hadn't written it yourself. And now I'll tell you something you'll really like. At this book fair they will have real live authors – and a badge-making machine."

The lower forms went down to the Book Fair in supervised groups. The Fifth Year, as befitted the enormous strides that they had made in self-discipline during the summer holidays, were left to find their own way. Rodney attached himself wordlessly to a sauntering cluster comprising the visual cream of his class: Eddie Hobson, known as Hobbers, and his three young ladies: Anna Miles, Katy Matthews, and Liz Salkey, the one with the eyes, the one with the ankles, the one with absolutely

9

everything in between and all of it, by popular repute, promised to horrible Hobbers. Rodney suspected that they considered themselves too pretty to be seen associating with his own plain person, but knowing that if they told him to go away he would neither answer nor go away, they allowed him to slouch behind them to the hall.

Inside, they looked round in disdain.

"It's all kids' stuff," Katy said. "Little baby books and posters. Fenton's pulled a fast one on us."

"All this way and nothing to read," mourned Hobbers, who had never yet been caught in possession of a book. "Can't even read old King these days, since Fenton debadged him. I bet you took the filthy ones off, King."

"He never had any filthy ones," Anna said.

"He did," said Hobbers, quietly, "only he's so thick he doesn't know they were filthy." Liz, lovely Liz, said nothing at all.

Rodney set off round the hall. There were five live authors, all looking repellently like teachers, several thousand books, a man flogging literary T-shirts, and the badge-making machine. The queue for badges stretched down one side of the hall, and Rodney attached himself to the tail of it, feeling like Gulliver in Lilliput among so many first school children, all squeaking like unoiled roller skates. Fenton had reminded everyone to bring money with which to buy books, to be signed by the live authors. Rodney had brought two pounds with which he bought ten badge blanks. The little kids all round him were scrawling their names in orange or turquoise, and drawing Dracula, with bats. Rodney brought his A+ for Art and Design into play. He heard Liz addressing Hobbers.

"Let's both get a badge made. I'll have your name and you have mine."

"Get out of it," said the gallant Hobbers. "I might get taken for King in a bad light."

"I'll make you a badge, Liz," Rodney said, suddenly, before he had time to lose courage. "What would you like?"

"You stick to scribbling on your own walls, beautiful," Hobbers said obscurely, with throaty threatening noises, and Liz was hauled away, badgeless.

Monday lunchtime brought Fenton and Rodney together again.

"I fear we're going to see a lot of each other this term," Fenton sighed. "You're sailing perilously close to the wind, King. You don't want a total embargo on your cargo, do you?"

Rodney had been practising a new gesture over the weekend. He raised his left eyebrow.

"ROD AGAINST RACISM I like," said Fenton. "ROD AGAINST THE BOMB is morally impeccable. However, NO FLIES ON ROD is another matter. When I told you to take the bloody things off your jacket I didn't mean that you should put them anywhere else. That scrum at break, round the coffee machine, was largely caused by your reading public, King, on its hands and knees, perusing your jeans. What the hell is that on the back of your neck?" Rodney turned round so that Fenton could see the badge on his collar: KING'S HEAD. NO COACHES.

"Exquisite lettering. I said nothing on your back."

"It's under my hair, unless I look down," Rodney protested.

"It's under your *back* hair," Fenton said. "Edit yourself, King."

Rodney edited himself drastically, removing KING CAN SERIOUSLY DAMAGE YOUR HEALTH, NO U TURNS, NO S BENDS, NO Y FRONTS and DANGER, CONCEALED EXIT from their carefully chosen sites, leaving only a striking model in severe black type on white, after the fashion of London Transport: WATCH THIS SPACE, which he wore until Wednesday.

WATCH THIS SPACE provoked a gratifying curiosity among his readership. Even Hobbers and his little harem displayed some interest in his frontage. When public response had, he judged, reached its peak, he removed WATCH THIS SPACE and pinned another badge in its place.

"Oh look – a new one," Anna cried, homing in on it. A moment later she recoiled and walked back to Katy with an affronted expression.

"What does it say?" Katy asked. "Something disgusting?"

"Read it yourself, if you want to know," Anna said, sulkily. Katy stood up and approached Rodney's table. Rodney obligingly angled his shoulder the better to display his lapel. Katy leaned toward him, flushed, and backed off. Finally Liz, curious in spite of herself, wandered over.

"What does it say, Rod?"

"You wouldn't want to read it," Rodney said, and folded his arms over his chest. "I've got a different one for you." He was aware of Hobbers, glowering over by the window in an attitude of Neanderthal aggression. "You can look at it later on."

"Can't I see it now?"

"Not here." Rodney looked shocked. "See you at

break – outside the library." He rose swiftly and went out.

"Well then," Hobbers demanded, with menaces, "what did it say? What's his badge of the week or flavour of the month this time, then?"

"I don't know. He wouldn't let me look," Liz said.

"You keep away from him and his badges," Hobbers said. "I don't know what the attraction is, the boring little git."

"He's funny," she said.

"Funny?"

"Anyway, attraction's not something you'd know much about, is it?" Liz said, shortly. She joined Katy and Anna on their way to class.

"Did you see what it said?" Katy asked.

"No. What did it say?"

"IF YOU CAN READ THIS YOU ARE TOO CLOSE," Anna snapped.

Liz smiled. "Oh."

"What are you grinning about?"

"I suppose that's why he wouldn't let me read it," Liz said.

At break she went to find Rodney outside the deserted library. He was there, his lapel vacant, and wearing a tie. On the knot of the tie was a badge.

"It better not be something foul," Liz warned him.

Rodney mimed affronted innocence. Would I do that? asked his arching eyebrows.

Liz leaned toward him and studied the legend: READ THE SMALL PRINT. "Is that all?"

"Of course it isn't. *Read* the small print."

"I can see that. What small print?"

"Round the edge," said Rodney.

13

"That?" Liz peered, inches away. "That squiggle? I thought it was the border."

"It's not a squiggle. It's small print: very small print."

"Get away, I can't read that."

"You can if you come near enough," Rodney said, and held his breath, praying that he had not taken the onions out of last night's hamburger in vain.

"Is it going to be worth it?"

"It's for *you*."

"And it's not something filthy?"

"Liz," Rodney said, solemnly, "if you don't trust me, you'll never find out what it says, will you?"

She was squinting past his chin, now. "I still can't read it."

"You'll have to come closer, then, won't you?" and he closed his eyes, saying silently, Oh God, make it work, and when he opened them again she was still there, right under his nose, reading the world's smallest love letter round the edge of his tenth badge. He thought, I wonder what would happen if I kissed her, and wished he could ask, but he had run out of badges.

Jan Mark: "I do not wear badges myself, but I collect them for my son, who does not wear them either – he just likes having *them, and it was at a book fair, of which institution this story features a very unfair description, that I first saw a badge-making machine in action. Incidentally, it's not true that all writers look like teachers, although a number have been teachers, and some still are. I never wrote any books while I was teaching. I was too tired."*

WOOF
Jan Dean

"They all know me here. I'm the one who barks."
The thought pleased Kevin as he monkeyed up the
drainpipe and onto the flat roof of the canteen.

"Can you see, Kev?" Colin and the others from
3C were at the back of the building, ready to run to
any of a dozen other hiding places if discovery
threatened.

Kevin crouched by the guttering. Three old tennis balls lay in a line by the top of the downspout.
There was a low wall surrounding the edge of the
roof. Kevin peered over it towards the science block
doors. Two men walked out into the yard.

"Grrrwuff!" Kevin yapped, twice.

"Teachers," Colin translated. "Two of them.
Who, Kev?"

"Yip-yip-yip."

"Mr Tanner." Colin relayed the information.

"Grr. Grrruff. Grrruff."

"And Mr Southall."

Kevin began to bark loudly, urgently.

"They're coming," Colin said, "Scatter! Are you
with us, Kev?"

But Kevin was capering now, across the roof like
a wild thing; half ape, half wolf. He leaped and
growled and flailed his arms like a manic windmill.
Then he stopped, directed an artfully inquisitive
stare at the masters in the yard and pranced sideways, slowly, each movement precise and delicate.
Next he cocked his head, swayed forward and
rested his knuckles on the low wall at the edge.
Controlled and deft, he stretched out his neck,
arched back his head and howled.

Mr Tanner and Mr Southall, stock still from the
start of the performance, looked at each other.

"Oh my God," sighed Tanner.

"Why us?" Southall muttered. "There's no use
talking to that boy. No use at all. Why the hell
couldn't someone else have found him?"

Together they moved towards the canteen.
Kevin bobbed down.

"He must be joking," said Tanner. "Hide-and-
Seek now. Perhaps he hopes we'll pretend we
haven't seen him."

"You can never tell what Mayfield hopes."
Southall sounded tired.

They stopped six feet from the wall and shouted
up.

"Mayfield! We know you're up there. Come on
down!"

There was no reply, but two tennis balls bombed
from the roof. They struck the tarmac hard and
bounced around them maddeningly.

"Mayfield!"

Kevin rose from his hiding place, mock-sheepish,
the third and oldest tennis ball in his mouth. He
climbed down.

He stood limply by the drainpipe and said

nothing. His shoulders sagged and his head drooped. He looked mournfully from Mr Southall to Mr Tanner, dribbling gently onto the dirty grey fur of the tennis ball.

"Right, Kevin, where should you be?"

Kevin stared at them with spaniel eyes, but said nothing. The tennis ball bulged from his jaws like a huge gum-boil.

"Drop that," said Tanner, bored and irritated by Kevin's dumb resistance.

The ball fell and rolled wetly to Tanner's feet.

"Now, how about some answers? What are you doing out here?" asked Southall.

"Wuff!" said Kevin.

"That's enough," said Tanner, "we'll have some sensible answers, if you don't mind. Now, what are you doing here and where should you be?"

Kevin could see the strain in Tanner's eyes, knew he was reining in his anger.

"They don't like that," he thought. "If he loses his temper and I keep mine, who's the mad one then?"

"I'm not prepared to wait all day." Tanner was snappy now. "What the hell are you playing at?"

It was almost equal terms now. Tanner felt it too, felt himself dragged outside the careful list of don'ts that he stood for. Kevin had won.

In belling triumph, Kevin bayed like a hound. Tanner wanted to smash his head from his shoulders, shut him up once and for all. He stepped forward then drew back, hot and aware.

"For God's sake take him away before I do something I'll regret." He turned away.

"Come on, Wolf Man," said Southall.

From the other side of the yard, Jack Crockett saw

it all. He stood at the Craft Room window and watched the whole thing. When the yard was empty again he turned back to his bench.

"Mayfield," he sneered as he picked up his hammer. "Bested by Mayfield."

He raised the hammer and let it fall. The iron would do as it was told.

In the corridor outside the Head's room Kevin barked at the school secretary.

"He's not right, that boy," she said to the typist as they counted and bagged dinner money. "He wants locking up."

Kevin watched her struggle her way from office to office, juggling files and duplicating paper. He growled softly whenever she came near.

Kevin disliked meeting the Head. He never knew quite where he stood. Dalton was too quick, too unlike the rest. At best he treated Kevin's barks as silence, at worst he barked first. It upset Kevin, left him empty.

The office door opened and the secretary edged past gingerly. Kevin rolled back his top lip into his most wolfish smile.

"Enter!" Mr Dalton hardly looked up as Kevin went in. "Again, Kevin? I thought we sorted out all this nonsense the last time."

"Sir."

"Right. Let's just go over this morning's escapade, shall we?"

Kevin was silent.

"First of all, *on the roof*. Now, you know the rules, Kevin, and I'm not going to waste my breath repeating them. The roof is out of bounds. Is that quite clear?"

"Sir."

"And as for your absence from maths during period two, well that's quite straightforward. Detention. This Thursday."

The interview was over. Mr Dalton waited for Kevin to go, but Kevin did not. He looked at Mr Dalton expectantly.

"Yes? Did you want to say something?"

"What about the other, Sir?" Kevin was eager, pushy.

"What? What other?"

"The barking, Sir." Admit it, he thought, admit that it's important.

"Oh, that. You must give me credit for some things, Kevin. No one could say I was without a sense of humour. Off you go." And then, as an afterthought,

"Woof-woof."

The break bell rang and Kevin left.

Outside in the yard a crowd of maths dodgers fed him gum. He had been a good decoy.

"Ta, Kev. Want a chew?"

He sat and begged, rolled over, played dead and snarled at outsiders who passed too close to the group. He revelled in it, fed on it. It was his voice, his name. They thought it was just a game, Mr Dalton, Tanner and Southall and the rest, but they were wrong.

Kevin grinned and rolled his eyes at a gang of fifth form girls. They giggled and he let his tongue loll over his teeth. Their giggling tightened into nervy laughter. He padded closer, pulled up sharply and sniffed. He singled out a small dark girl and moved towards her. He snuffled as he circled her, tasting the air.

"Get off," she said and tried to move away, but he had cut her off from the herd and now he barred her path.

"Shift!" She was angry now and swung her arm at his head.

Kevin yelped and cowered. He howled, long mournful howls, and padded quietly after the retreating girl.

"Bloody nut!" she shouted at him. "Go on, Kevin, back to your kennel."

Even the fifth form knew who he was.

In the staff room Jack Crockett fished for information.

"I hear you had a bit of bother with Mayfield."

Tanner was non-committal.

"Something and nothing."

"Oh, own up. You had a run-in with him, didn't you? Nothing wrong with that. Nothing to be ashamed of. They get away with murder, these boys. Standing there with 'you-can't-touch-me' grins all over their vicious little faces. Well it's time somebody did, I can tell you. It's time somebody did."

"Hardly appropriate for Mayfield." Southall was cold. "He's a clown, that's all."

Crockett mocked him. "Oh, that's right, pretend he's harmless, then you needn't do anything about him. All good clean fun, eh? He's baiting us. He incites indiscipline. That boy is trouble. He's got us with our backs against the wall."

"Oh, come on." Southall's quiet laughter was uncertain. "Aren't you going off the deep end a bit? The lad's a bit disturbing, I'll grant you, but he's hardly a threat."

20

Tanner wanted to agree; he'd no time for Crockett and his kind who passed nostalgia off as wisdom, but he could not. Tanner had stood face to face with Mayfield on Mayfield's ground.

"I think it's quite serious," Tanner said. "I think he really has a problem."

"Oh my God." Crockett's exasperation peaked. "Heaven defend me from psychologists!"

After break, Kevin lined up with the rest of the class outside the Metalwork Room. Jack Crockett bore down on them from the far end of the corridor. The snake of boys rippled and straightened. Crockett would not let them in if they lounged or strayed from the queue.

"Watch it, Kev. He's in a mood," Colin warned as they stood more or less to attention. Kevin glanced in Crockett's direction. Colin was right, he could tell by the walk. Crockett seemed on the verge of bouncing along, each step sprung with aggression. He looked along the line. It was their version of straight. But to Crockett the boots, the jackets, the haircuts all signalled decay. It was rot, the shuffle back to slime.

"Psychology," he seethed as he unlocked the door and the boys filed in. "Just a minute," he said, soft as lead, as Kevin moved past him in the doorway. "Stand out at the front. I want a word."

It was time.

The rest of the boys were standing by their benches, craft aprons folded in front of them, when Jack Crockett closed the door. Michael Watts had taken his half-made money box from the cupboard and was anxious to begin.

"Stand still, Watts. What's that on your bench?"

21

"It's my work, Sir."

"I don't remember giving permission for boys to get out their work."

"No, Sir."

"Put it away, Watts."

"Yes, Sir."

"Now, what have we here?" He looked at Kevin carefully, as if he were a model he was going to demonstrate to the group.

"Ah yes, Kevin Mayfield. The Incredible Barking Boy."

The class tittered.

"Known in school and staff room as the Wolf Man of the Junior Forms."

The laughter swelled. Kevin liked it.

"Fancy yourself, don't you, dog-boy?"

The challenge thrummed in the air. Kevin felt it. He bunched his arms and hands into dangling paws and began to pant.

Crockett took one step forward and snorted his disgust. Kevin looked at him, cocked his leg like a dog at a post and launched into bursts of frantic yelping.

Crockett roared. "Enough!"

The background cackles ceased, smothered by the violence of the shout. For a second the whole room froze to a film still. Kevin saw the fine mist of spit from Crockett's shout as clearly as splinters of glass, as if an empty milk bottle had exploded in the air between them. In the stillness Kevin knew, too late, that this was different. Tanner had despised his rage, Crockett did not; he would not step back, he welcomed the anger and the heat. He would not lose his temper, lose control, lose the edge, but simply use it, like the furnace, to bend or break.

Suddenly it was all action, the film rolled on in an instant. Crockett had him by the shoulder and was shaking him. Each thrust shocked his spine. The breath was being knocked out of him. His joints screamed, he screamed. Crockett let go.

"It's time," he hissed. "It's time you learned. You've skated through long enough. We've humoured you long enough. Well, you're going to be house-trained. Do you hear? House-trained."

He picked up a steel bar from the bench and dropped it by Kevin's feet.

"Fetch," he said.

Kevin did not move. What was he trying to do?

"Fetch." His voice was softer now, and as menacing as mink. Kevin looked; Crockett was six foot and between him and the door. He bent to pick up the bar.

"No, Kevin, not like that. Like you fetch Daddy's slippers, like you fetch a bone."

Crockett was a wall with fists. Kevin fetched the bar.

"Good dog, Mayfield. Good dog."

The class were silent now, and frightened.

"Watts, bring me that grease."

The lid resisted at first, then gave way to Crockett's twisting with a soft plop. The dark grease glistened. He dug deep into the can and scooped out a glutinous lump. He smiled at the mass in his hand, savouring the weight and the texture. Lovingly he larded the rod and dropped it again at Kevin's feet.

"Fetch," he almost sang.

"Sir?" Watts was pale.

"Yes, Michael? Do you want to play?"

Michael bit his lip.

"Right-oh, Kevin. Fetch." The word rang like a gin-trap. Crockett gripped the back of Kevin's neck, working his fingers as if to find purchase between spine and muscle. Kevin squirmed, but he could not wrench away. Crockett straightened his arm and, relentless and smooth as a slow-motion piston, drove Kevin down.

"Sir!" Michael Watts felt sick.

Crockett was almost kneeling on Kevin's back, shoving his face into the filth.

"Fetch! Fetch!" Such a quiet command. Crockett bubbled like the acid bath.

"No!" Kevin turned his head. Crockett forced it back and down, down onto the bar.

"That's right." The whisper drilled into him. "Rub his nose in it! Rub his nose in it!"

The pain in his neck shot electric flicks down his arms. He groaned. His teeth banged against the bar. He opened his mouth.

Kevin stood mute, sick with the taste of grease. Crockett had taken his music, stolen it, taken his voice just as surely as if he had ripped it out of his throat. Now Kevin was just like all the others.

Jack Crockett turned to the class. He had made his point.

"Get out your work," he said.

It was several months later when Jack Crockett had his accident. He was tidying up at the end of a lesson when he knocked over a naked light and there was an explosion. Somehow the tap of a gas bottle had been switched on and the gas, heavier than air, had sunk and filled the blacksmith's hearth. The flame fell and it blew; first the soft sigh, then the dull boom. Mr Crockett was thrown twenty feet across the room.

Michael Watts went for help.

Kevin sat quietly remembering the exact sound as the first flame touched the gas. "Whoof!" he said inside his head, "Whoof!"

Then the room was full of people sorting things out and sending the boys away.

There was a spate of accidents around that time; a fire in the Domestic Science Room and a small but colourful bang in the Chemistry Lab. Mr Dalton was worried. He was considering extra fire drills when he met Kevin by the boiler room.

"Ah, Mayfield. Seen the Caretaker?"

"No, Sir. Sorry, Sir."

"Not to worry. Not seen you in my room for a while. Good. Glad to see you're settling down."

Then, as an afterthought:

"Woof-woof!"

Kevin looked blank. "I don't do that any more, Sir," he said, and smiled.

Jan Dean: "All sorts of things can start a story; people tell each other stories all the time. I listen when people talk to me, I eavesdrop on the train, I use what I hear, adapt it, explore it, fleshing out events with feeling and motives. 'Woof' sprang from two separate ideas and I used the bones of the story to say something about tensions in schools. I hope it never comes true."

SCHOOL PLAY
Chrys Bensted

It was the custom at our school (heaven knows who
started it) for the Fifth Years to put on a Christmas
entertainment for the rest of the school and the
parents. Last year I had the doubtful privilege of
getting it all together. Of course, that was all the
fault of Jones the Steam, our Welsh fireball of a
Drama teacher.

"Barnes," she said, collaring me dramatically on
the way out of Assembly, "Barnes, I want you to
write the Fifth Year play. Nothing heavy, mind.
Something funny. God knows, we all need something to laugh at these days." She always called me
Barnes – in fact, everyone did. Sometimes I almost
forgot I was christened Amanda.

Anyway I racked my brains (such as they were)
and finally came up with the Barnes Special Version of *Cinderella*. Panto's always good for a giggle,
and most people were willing to take part. The only
snag was finding a Prince Charming. I wanted a
boy, and they all flatly refused. Too wet, they said,
so in the end I had to persuade Andy to take the
part.

Andy was easily the nicest boy in our year – and I
don't mean that he was soppy. He was just totally
good-natured. He never minded the friendly teas-
ing of his mates, nor the fact that they called him
'Randy Andy' – a nickname without a grain of
truth in it. Andy was tall, lanky and freckled, with
a grin that spread from ear to ear. He was also
game for anything, so I tackled him one lunchtime
in the school canteen. I must admit he was unen-
thusiastic, to say the least.

"What me? Play Prince Charming? Are you nuts,
Barnes?" he said indistinctly through a mouthful
of egg-and-chips. "I mean, have a heart – do I *look*
the part?"

"Oh, that doesn't matter," I said impatiently.
"It's all meant to be a big joke anyway."

"Well, thanks a lot! Look, have you really asked
everyone else?"

"Everyone. You're my last hope, Andy."

"Oh, all right, then. But only if I get to kiss
Sonia."

"I'll see what I can wangle into the script," I said,
and disappeared before he could change his mind.

Sonia just had to be our Cinderella. I couldn't
really have chosen anyone else. She was tall and
dramatic, with dazzling blonde hair, and her figure
had what the books call 'generous curves'. In fact,
she was a stunner, or would have been, if her
manner hadn't been so overpowering. It was her
boast that she'd been asked out by almost every boy
in our year, but I knew for a fact that most of the
boys thought she was a pain, despite her obvious
good points. She just never could stop acting. Every
movement was planned for maximum effect. It
really was a question of overkill, but she would

make a great Cinderella – mostly because she would take the part so seriously that everyone would think she must be playing it for laughs. I knew she wouldn't be, and I also knew she would be none too pleased to have Andy play the male lead.

"Him? Prince Charming?" she scoffed when I told her later that day. "He's got about as much sex-appeal as – as a stale rock-cake!"

"It is meant to be funny, Sonia," I protested. "I'm sure he'll be great. Oh, by the way, – Jonesy's persuaded Mr Winters to help us with rehearsals."

"Mr Winters!" Sonia breathed the name reverently through parted lips. "*He* can help me rehearse any time!"

I said no more. Mr Winters was our new English teacher, and I must admit he was something. Tall, blond, about twenty-three, and incredibly shy – at least with us girls. We all fancied him like mad, but no one more than Sonia. She'd suddenly begun talking about how silly boys were compared with mature men, and she was always trying to bump into him in the corridor, or stay behind in English. He didn't seem to cotton on at first, but after a while went out of his way to avoid her, much to our amusement.

"Mr Winters doesn't seem very impressed by your tactics," I said one day while we were changing for PE.

"That's all you know," Sonia said mysteriously. "Actually Graham – I mean Mr Winters – and I are very good friends out of school."

"Oh, come off it, Sonia," I said. "You're just boasting again. He doesn't come near you . . ."

"Of course he doesn't!" she said. "He's too embarrassed. He wouldn't want anyone to know!"

"Know what?" I was half believing her now. She was quite convincing.

"Know that he's taken me out, of course. But don't tell anyone, Barnes. This is strictly between the two of us."

Well of course my curiosity was aroused, and just as she'd planned I *did* tell someone else – several people in fact. Rumours flew thick and fast. Had he really asked her out? She was sixteen, after all, and it made sense that he would avoid her in school, though surely she should have done the same? Some girl said she'd seen them together in the High Street. Someone else swore they'd been in the Red Lion pub two nights ago. When questioned, Sonia said nothing, but just smiled her mysterious smile.

In the middle of all this intrigue, I battled on with the pantomime. It was shaping up nicely, and I was really quite pleased. The day of the dress-rehearsal came at last, and all went well, apart from a slight technical hitch. Andy, who was looking rather green about the gills, and complaining that he felt lousy, added a few extra laughs to our final scene by mistakenly carrying on the wrong glass slipper. Sonia had rather large feet, and the perspex Christmas reject which Andy took on didn't go anywhere near her. She was furious, of course, and gave him a mouthful of choice language in a piercing stage-whisper, which had us all rolling about. Poor Andy looked really crushed – as well as ill – and couldn't stop apologizing afterwards. I think he really liked her.

The next day was The Big One. Andy was looking worse than ever, and said he thought he had 'flu.

"But you'll be all right for tonight, won't you?

You can't let me down, Andy!"

"Oh, shut up, Barnes, I feel terrible, and your nagging at me isn't going to improve matters."

"Think of being kissed by Sonia," I said hopefully.

I won't say what he said, but it was rude, and quite unlike him, and he stomped off, looking miserable. I feared the worst, and by afternoon break my fears were confirmed. Jonesy came up, breathing smoke and fire.

"Barnes, Andrew Stone has a raging temperature, and has had to be sent home; what are we going to do?"

I thought it was a nerve putting it all on my shoulders. "We'll have to find someone to understudy for him, but I can't think of anyone who knows all the lines."

Jonesy perked up a bit. "Now, there's an idea. I bet Mr Winters knows most of the part – he's helped with enough rehearsals."

In fact I'd hardly noticed him at rehearsals, but that was probably because he'd been keeping a low profile – on account of Sonia, no doubt. Jonesy shot off like an arrow from a bow, and came back ten minutes later with an air of grim triumph.

"It's all right, Barnes. Graham – Mr Winters – has agreed to stand in for Andrew."

Poor fool! I wondered what she'd done to him to get him to agree! Still, that wasn't my worry. I decided to break the news to Sonia.

"Andy's got 'flu," I said, as we trooped into Biol, our last lesson. "Your friend Graham is taking the part."

"My – you mean Mr Winters?" Sonia's mouth dropped open. "Are you joking?"

"No, deadly serious. So don't distract him too much with your fatal charms." I was to remember that remark later.

Sonia said nothing more, but she looked quite white all through Biol, like someone in a bad dream, and didn't even flinch at the eyeball we were taking apart.

I didn't see her again till we were all gathered in the dressing-room backstage. She rushed in late, looking distraught, grabbed her first-act costume and rushed out again. I decided she was best left alone, and went to see how well the seats were filling up. I was just sneaking back when a voice said, "Excuse me. Can you tell me where I should be sitting?" I looked up to see a very pretty girl, about twenty, with long black hair and very shapely legs. I didn't recognize her from Adam. Someone's sister, I supposed.

"Er, whose ..." I began, but just then Jonesy came steaming up. "Susie, how lovely! Mind, you're in for a surprise! Your fiancé is playing Prince Charming!"

"Is he? That should be funny." And the girl grinned at me, and went to sit in the 'Staff Reserved' seats.

Fiancé? She was engaged to Graham Winters! So all the rumours were false, and Sonia had been having us on. Or had she ... ?

The panto started and all went well. Everyone laughed loudly in the right places, and sometimes in the wrong ones, but who cared? In the interval before the ballroom scene, I noticed that Cinders was missing. "Where's Sonia? She should be ready by now."

"Haven't seen her." Gill Honeyman, the Wicked

Stepmother, looked surprised. "Thought she'd be all ready to dazzle Graham – ah, here she comes. Hey, Sonia, that's not your ball costume!"

"No it isn't!" I said icily. "*What* is *that*?"

"Well," said Sonia airily, "you said play it for laughs, so that's what I am doing." She was wearing a white satin sheath-dress with a *very* low neckline, and a skirt split as high as it could decently go – also a white feather boa. Her hair, the only concession, was swept up, but somehow it only made the whole thing look worse – or better, whichever way you looked at it. I knew how Jonesy and the Head would look at it, and I knew who'd get the blame.

"You can't go on like that!" I snapped. "You'll ruin everything!"

"Just you try to stop me," said Sonia sweetly, and at that moment Jonesy called out, "Come on, they're ready for you." I rushed round to the side of the stage, and crouched in the wings. Graham Winters was looking very handsome in his Prince Charming get-up. I caught sight of Susie in the second row, and felt all goose-pimply.

"The Princess of Peppermintia!" announced the herald, and Sonia swept on stage. The effect was electrifying. The audience, literally, held its breath. Well, she did look a knockout. She went up to Prince Charming and curtsied, as far as the split skirt would allow.

"Your Highness," she breathed reverently. And Graham Winters, forced to look at her at last, just couldn't take his eyes off her. He was riveted. I don't think I've ever seen anyone stare quite so blatantly. Then, to my amazement, a deep burning blush spread over Sonia's cheeks. I thought she was going to cry. She suddenly looked like an awkward schoolgirl, despite the clothes.

"H . . . h . . . how do you do, Princess?" stuttered Prince Charming. "I . . . I . . ." He stopped, looked round helplessly, and the audience went into hysterics. Even the Head was laughing.

"I am pleased to make your acquaintance!" hissed the prompter. Mr Winters looked blank for a moment, then seemed to recall where he was.

The rest of the play went OK and I rushed to the dressing-room afterwards to congratulate my cast. Sonia was furiously stripping off make-up.

"How *dare* he. How *dare* he look at me like that!" she stormed. "In front of all those people . . . I could have died!"

"But you wanted him to," I said reasonably, "or you'd never have gone on dressed up like that."

"Dirty old man, how dare he?" she sobbed. "I hate him! He ruined it!"

"Well, I shouldn't think Susie enjoyed it much either," I couldn't help saying sarcastically.

"Who the hell's Susie, anyway?" Sonia mopped at her face with a tissue.

"Graham Winters's fiancée, of course. I would have thought you knew she was here, as you're *such* good friends!" I dodged the glass slipper hurled at my head . . . but only just!

Surprisingly, everything went back to normal very quickly. Jonesy was charming to me about the pantomime. No mention was made of the Sonia incident, and we'd sold a record number of tickets, which pleased the Head. Andy came back in a few days and had to be told the whole story. Sonia was very quiet for a while, but soon found herself a new interest – the boy who'd moved in next door was apparently 'an ace with bikes'. So what was the next role for Sonia – Hell's Angel?

Graham and Susie came to the end-of-term disco, looking shy, sweet and in love. I dared Sonia to ask Mr Winters for a dance and – what a nerve – she did! What's more, he accepted! Well, as Andy said as he trod on my foot for the fiftieth time that evening – anything's good for a laugh.

Chrys Bensted: "I always longed to play Cinderella at school, but the big chance finally came when I was teaching – my Fifth Year 'Cinders' was suddenly struck down, and I had to stand in for her. I was terrified, but Prince Charming, her classmate, saved the day; despite the cackles of laughter from his mates offstage, he managed not only to remember his own lines but to prompt me as well! I have never wanted to be Cinderella since!"

A DAY TOO LATE
Pat Ayinde

Sarah sat on the low wall that ran along the side of the fish pond, near the school entrance. She watched the crowd of girls jostling through the iron gates, looking for one of her friends. Suddenly someone grabbed her.

"Sarah!" shrieked Joanne. "You'll fall in if you don't watch out. Ask me how last night went, then."

Sarah looked affectionately at her friend. Joanne sat down untidily on the edge of the fish pond, her bag in serious danger of falling in the water. But she was engrossed in the story of her evening out, and did not really mind what happened to her books.

"Hi, you two." It was Yvette, standing in front of them in that casual way of hers, as if she did not care whether they noticed her or not.

"Hello, Yvette," said Sarah. "Joanne's telling me about last night and John."

"Start at the beginning again then," said Yvette. "But get a move on. It's registration in two minutes."

"Well, I can't tell the *whole* story," started Joanne. As she spoke Susan ran up.

"Hello," she puffed. "I've got to slim. I'm sure I'm overweight. I just ran up the road from the bus stop and I feel awful!"

The other three laughed. Susan was already the thinnest of them all and she was always talking about diets – *and* she ate like a horse.

"Come on," said Joanne. "Let's go and get registered. We've got Mrs Fairfield and work experience this morning, and you know how she nags if we're late."

"Just remember that you are visitors, and that the Matron of the Home is doing us a favour. It's most important that you behave well; this community experience is part of your exam, and if you get turned out because of bad behaviour, then that's it as far as the exam is concerned." Mrs Fairfield looked round the class expectantly, but nobody had any comments so she continued, "I hope you will bear in mind what we have discussed in our lessons with regard to old people . . . most old people, that is. You are not visiting these old ladies and gentlemen to tell them your views about your favourite pop group. You are there to listen and be a friend."

Joanne nudged Yvette, who was sitting next to her. "Are you playing bulldog at dinner-time?" Yvette shrugged, "Shhh, I'm listening." "But are you?" insisted Joanne. Mrs Fairfield glared at them and went on,

"You may get bored, they may say things you disagree with, they may even be rude to you – but it is part of the experience to learn how to cope with other people's nastiness."

"Do you understand what she's talking about?" Sarah hissed into Susan's ear.

"Any comments?" asked Mrs Fairfield.

"Yes," said Susan. "Like my old Gran – I get that experience every day . . . 'Here you are, Gran, I've brought you some toffee.' 'You know I can't eat toffee without my teeth.' But she eats the lot just the same."

"Yes, Susan, that's how it goes sometimes. They can be very awkward." Mrs Fairfield smiled politely.

Just then the bell rang and Mrs Fairfield gathered up her bag and books and left the classroom. The girls took out their crisps and between mouthfuls discussed the prospect of visiting the Old People's Home.

Fifteen minutes later, Joanne, Yvette, Susan and Sarah, who were all going to the same Old People's Home, were walking down the road, glad to be out of the school and in the sunshine.

"I'm nervous," said Sarah. "Suppose the old lady I get is . . ."

"You might get an old man," interrupted Joanne. Sarah gave her a friendly push, and the four of them walked through the gate and up the short drive to the entrance.

Mrs Clarke, the Matron of the Home, met them at the door. She was a tall thin lady with an attractive smile.

"Good morning, girls. I'm Mrs Clarke, the Matron. I'll show you where to hang your coats, and then you can come through and meet the residents. I know Mrs Fairfield will have prepared you well; she's been sending her girls to visit my old people for years now." She showed the girls a small cloakroom and waited while they tidied their hair and put their clothes straight. "Well now, girls," she said, "I will introduce you each to one old lady or gentleman and you will visit the same one each week: the idea is that you should be a *regular* visitor. It doesn't matter if you hardly speak to each other, as long as the old folk can look forward to your visit every week, and depend on your arrival. These old people are the ones who hardly ever get any visitors." Mrs Clarke led the way up the passage to the day room.

"What a terrible way to live," whispered Sarah to Susan.

"Why don't they get any visitors?" demanded Joanne of the Matron.

"Well," she said, pausing at the entrance to the day room. "Their relatives and friends may be dead, or perhaps living far away, even abroad; or in a few cases they're just not interested."

"I think that's awful," muttered Sarah.

The day room was big and light, with easy chairs scattered around, and French windows leading into a garden – the whole place looked pleasant and airy. A number of old ladies and gentlemen were seated in chairs in the room, and others could be seen out in the garden. Two men were playing dominoes and one woman was reading, but most of them were just sitting, staring into space. One or two looked up as the girls entered. Sarah noticed one old lady busily occupied pulling threads from the blanket that covered her knees, and the girl's heart sank. What *was* she to say? At that moment she couldn't think of a single thing that might interest them. But then Mrs Fairfield's voice switched on inside her head, "You are there to listen".

"I hope I get a talkative one," thought Sarah. She knew that her three companions could all talk without giving it a thought. Already Susan and Yvette had been introduced to their old people and were sitting down, making lively comments and getting smiling answers. Mrs Clarke led Joanne and Sarah to two old ladies sitting on the far side of the room. She introduced Joanne to one of them and then turned to Sarah and said in a quiet voice, "I'm going to ask you to sit with Mrs Miles. She's not only a bit deaf, as many old people are, but she's also blind. Now don't let that worry you; she's a lively old stick and she'll talk you into the ground." Sarah's heart rose encouragingly. "Thank goodness," she thought. "I can just sit and listen."

"On the other hand," went on Mrs Clarke, "you must remember that with her, just sitting and smiling or nodding is no use; hold her hand, let her feel that you're there; make the occasional noise, even if it's only a cough."

Mrs Clarke smiled at Sarah and turned to Mrs Miles to introduce them. She touched the old lady lightly on the shoulder.

"I have someone come to see you, Mrs Miles," she shouted. Sarah felt embarrassed at the loud voice and looked around, expecting everyone in the room to be staring at them, but no one was.

The old lady in the chair turned her face towards the sound and smiled. "Oh, Mrs Clarke," she exclaimed. "I'm glad you've come over. I wanted to tell you that I don't want any potatoes at lunch. Those spuds we had yesterday were bad, y'know. Made me feel quite funny, they did." Mrs Clarke raised her eyes to the ceiling, but merely said, "Right. Now this is . . ." She looked at Sarah.

"I'm Sarah," said the girl to Mrs Miles and copying Mrs Clarke reached out and touched the old lady. Mrs Miles caught her hand and pulled her down to sit in the chair beside her. Mrs Clarke smiled once more at Sarah and left her to it.

"Sarah," said the old lady, still holding Sarah's hand trapped. "That's a pretty name. Old Testament. You're not Jewish, are you?"

"Well, no, I'm . . ." began Sarah, but Mrs Miles continued heedlessly.

"Not that I've got anything against the Jews, mind; good and bad everywhere, that's what I always say. What my old man used to say, too, before he was pushing up the daisies." She gave a sigh, let go of Sarah's hand and began to fiddle with her wedding ring. Sarah saw that her hands were calloused and the line markings on her fingers and thumbs were outlined in dirt, which was ingrained from years of labour. The fingers of her right hand were twisting the wedding ring, and moving it up and down; not that it would go very far up – over the years her fingers had become fatter and now the ring could not be removed. "My hubby – he was lovely; bit fond of the booze, mind, but he was good at heart. Never raised a hand to me or the kids. And he sweated blood to give us a home." Mrs Miles heaved another deep sigh and Sarah felt she ought to say something.

"How many children have you got?" she shouted.

"They're very good here, you know," went on Mrs Miles. She did not seem to have heard Sarah's question. "Give us good grub they do; and we have the wireless, and I listen to the telly sometimes. My Lucy, now, that's my youngest – she's in Australia – well, she was a great one for the books; she couldn't understand why I never took any interest; not that it'd be much use to me now. Here's her last letter. You can read it to me." From her pocket Mrs Miles drew out a blue airmail letter, very creased and grubby looking. Sarah took it and opened it. The letter was four months old. She began reading loudly, "Dear Mum, How are you ..." Mrs Miles sat nodding, smiling at her distant daughter's doings and news.

"You read nice, dear," she said, when Sarah had finished. "You could even get a job on the BBC. Lovely letter, but I wish she was here. Australia's so far away. All those foreigners and strange places. Do you know, there're black people that are still living in the Stone Age, going round half naked and that. I think it's disgusting. And then they come over here, fill up the houses and jobs and think they've got a right to it. Before I came to this place, I had a black woman living next door to me – used to visit me here till they moved to Wales. Anyway she brought me in some of their food, like what they eat; often used to bring stuff in she did – said she thought of me like I was her mum back in her country." Here Mrs Miles paused to laugh, and Sarah opened her mouth to speak but Mrs Miles beat her to it. "And one time when she came in she was moaning about how her hubby had lost his job – as if he had a right to a job over here."

When Mrs Miles stopped to draw breath, Sarah could not think what to say, where to begin, which bit of history, geography, ethics or economics would most enlighten Mrs Miles.

"Mind you," Sarah's mind jerked back from the problem of what to say to the effort of listening, "I like their kids, with their big eyes and that. How about this for a joke – they're all wight while they're young." Mrs Miles roared laughing at her own humour, and while Sarah was still hesitating over what to say, Mrs Clarke appeared in the doorway of the day-room.

"Girls, you'd better be getting back now, or you'll be late for school dinner," she called.

Sarah leaned over Mrs Miles and shouted, "I've got to go now, but I'll be back next week."

Mrs Miles nodded. "You're a good girl," she said. "Thank you for coming. Can you just help me on with my slippers?"

Sarah knelt down in front of the old lady and drew the slippers out from under the chair. As Sarah put them on for her, Mrs Miles leant forward to pat her on the head, and felt the tight, springy hair of a black person. Her hand froze on the top of Sarah's curls. Her fingers, calloused and dirty, were nevertheless the sensitive fingers of a blind person, now learning for the first time something of the physical appearance of the girl who had sat so quietly listening to her. For those few precious seconds Mrs Miles the talkative could not say anything! Then she snatched her hand back as if Sarah's head were suddenly hot.

"Come on, Sarah," said Joanne. "Leave the miserable old sod, and let's get out of here."

"Goodbye, Mrs Miles," said Sarah, touching the old lady's shoulder. Then she left with her three friends.

"I don't know how you keep so cool," exploded Joanne as soon as they were out of the building. "I heard every word she said. You should've heard her," here she turned to Yvette and Susan, "telling

Sarah how black people go round half naked, and have no rights here, and telling some crummy joke." She turned and looked back at Sarah. "And you just sat there. Why didn't you *say* something?" Joanne was simply furious, striding along, her red hair blowing in the wind like an ancient warrior's, scowling at Sarah and any passer-by who happened to catch her eye.

"I was going to," replied Sarah, "but she talked so fast; and then I couldn't think what to say. You know what Mrs Fairfield always says . . ."

"They're the ones who feel insecure – educationally, economically or emotionally," chanted the three girls together, and then they all laughed and broke the tension.

"But seriously," went on Joanne, "what do you do when something like that happens to you, Yvette? You weren't born here. I mean, if someone says, 'Hey, Ginger,' or something to me, I get real mad and insult them back."

"Well," said Yvette, "I think it depends on who it is. I don't think I could've got mad with the old lady. She can't do anything to upset me in there. Someone on a bus or something, that'd be different. Like when someone mutters an insult in your ear, so that you look ridiculous if you try to pick an argument. Well, I just mutter some insult back, but in dialect. Then they know they've been insulted but they don't know what I've said. That really gets them going." Yvette smiled to herself, obviously remembering some occasion when she had thus got the better of someone. "Anyway," she went on, "They're not all like that. My old chap said that if he was sixty years younger he'd be taking me to the pictures tonight."

"That reminds me," said Susan, "you know that new art teacher; he said he was going to try something different this week; I wonder what he's got planned for us."

Mrs Miles sat quite still for a long time after Sarah had gone. She could not remember all she had said, but she knew that a lot of it had been insulting, now that she knew the kind of girl she had been talking to.

"Here, Emma," she turned to her near neighbour. "Are you there?"

"Yes," replied Emma. "You don't half open your mouth and put your foot in it, do you, Gladys?"

"Emma, was that girl, well – was she black?" Mrs Miles waited anxiously.

"Well, not exactly. She was one of those lighter skinned ones, very pretty mind you; and she didn't look too upset. But you've made an enemy out of my girl, Joanne. I can tell you, she was livid. A few more seconds and she'd've dotted you one. Comes of having red hair, I suppose."

Mrs Miles did not reply, but sat back thinking hard. If only she'd known, she'd have been more careful. If she could have seen the girl then she wouldn't have said all those things. Maybe they are foreigners, but some of them are nice and friendly. Help you more than your own people, some of them. Look at Mrs Whatsit next door. Always popping in, always friendly and cheerful – she knew what it was like to have relatives living a long way away. They're not really so bad, after all. And it's not nice to go on at people the way she'd done.

All through her lunch Mrs Miles was unusually

quiet, except to complain at the end of the first course that she didn't know why they'd stopped giving her potatoes in this place. That afternoon Mrs Miles planned her apology. Next week she would explain to Sarah that she hadn't meant all those things. She would say "sorry" and hold her hand to show that she liked her. If only she had something to give her. Mrs Miles sat, thinking about the contents of her locker: not much there to appeal to a young girl. Of course, there was the crochet hook – Mrs Miles had been an expert once. Yes, that was it! She'd give Sarah the crochet hook and some wool she'd still got. She knew from the wireless that crochet was all the rage. Mrs Miles was excited by her plan. The next day she hunted through her locker and found the crochet hook she kept there. Then she asked Emma's advice about the colour of the wool she should choose. She even managed to persuade one of the orderlies to get her some pretty wrapping paper. Every day she took the crinkly parcel from her locker and felt it and imagined how she would apologize, and how friendly she and Sarah would become. She had no other visitors and her whole week was spent looking forward to Sarah's arrival.

"Come on," said Susan. "We'll be late." It was the following week and the four girls were once again walking to the Old People's Home.

" . . . but did he kiss you?" insisted Joanne.

"Mind your own business," said Sarah, blushing.

"Well, go on," said Joanne.

"Shut up," said Sarah, looking annoyed. "You don't tell me what you do with your boyfriend."

"My dear, I don't want to shock you," laughed Joanne.

"Here we are," said Yvette. "I've bought my chappy an ounce of tobacco."

"What are you going to say to your old biddy?" inquired Joanne of Sarah.

"Well," replied Sarah, "my mum said I should act as if nothing went wrong, and then if she mentions it I should say something quick and easy, like 'there's good and bad in all countries'. My mum said I couldn't start lecturing the old girl, and that I'd do more good by just being friendly. She said it's not as if she was one of my teachers, or someone whose attitude is really going to change things. She said . . ."

"I don't wonder you're so quiet," commented Joanne. "Your mum's got so much to say for herself."

They were greeted at the door by Mrs Clarke, who smiled at them, and then said to Sarah, "Would you come into my office for a moment, please, Sarah?"

Once inside, she turned to Sarah and said, "My dear, I'm afraid Mrs Miles died last night. She was very old, you know. I hope you won't let this upset you, and that you will feel able to chat to one of the other residents?" She looked inquiringly at Sarah, who nodded. As they turned to go, Sarah noticed Mrs Miles' slippers on top of a pile of other things, among which was what looked like someone's birthday present – a package wrapped in pretty paper. Sarah followed Mrs Clarke down the passage to the day-room.

Pat Ayinde: "When you can't see the person you are talking to (if you're blind, or talking on the telephone, for instance) you can't use physical appearance to make pre-judgements: you only have a voice to judge by. This idea intrigued me, because so often we are prejudiced by first impressions of what a person is wearing, how they look, or what colour their skin is."

THE
SLEEPING BEAUTY
OF ANTON P'NTARR

Sam McBratney

*(A light-hearted love story
set in the future)*

Author's Note:

*The action in this love-story happens a long way
from here, on a planet called Clemess Amara. When
the stars and several moons come out over Clemess
Amara, you can see in the southern sky a con-
stellation known as Hoth's Crib. Before you start the
story I have to tell you something about this fellow
Hoth.*

*Hoth and his wife lived in ancient times when
people were much the same as they are nowadays,
except that they didn't die. There was no sickness in
the world and everybody lived for ever. Poor old
Hoth was the one who changed all that.*

*Hoth's wife had a baby-sitting job. She nursed the
baby son of one of the top goddesses of that time,
Waina: and that's how the trouble started. Other
gods and goddesses were always trying to steal this
baby away from her, so Waina made a magic crib to
keep him safe. "While my baby sleeps," she said to
Hoth's wife, "you must always rock him in the crib
so that he is never still. So long as the baby is*

rocking, no harm can come to him. Attend carefully to this."

And indeed, Hoth's wife attended very carefully to that. One day she went to market, leaving the sleeping baby for her husband to look after. Silly old Hoth rocked the crib for a while, then nodded off in front of a roaring fire. When he woke up he found a wizened Changeling in the crib instead of Waina's pink and shiny new baby.

Poor Hoth tried to make a few excuses, but the gods never seem to listen when we mortals try to explain ourselves. "Your punishment shall be the creature in the Crib," Waina called out in a voice which seemed to roll down from the hills, "it shall grow and prosper, and in due time the peoples of this race shall meet with it face-to-face, and individually."

The Changeling grew, and prospered, and pursues us all to this day. Its name is Death.

How Anton P'ntarr loved that girl from the Inner-Space Menagerie! Every time he saw her his heart beat on his ribs as if it wanted to be let out of its cage.

He watched her feeding a Squit in its tank. The Squit's green head lay flat on the water rather like a pretty lily, and here ended the resemblance to flowers. Perishing Squits had teeth sharp enough to take your finger off. Then she checked the pressure in the cage inhabited by the hairy Gloop from the planet Perseus. This was a heavy-gravity planet and poor hairy Gloops exploded if the pressure dropped below 114 pounds per square inch. Pop! they went.

Anton P'ntarr wondered, by no means for the

first time, what had made this girl choose to work at the Inner-Space Menagerie. The school sent her here for two days a week as part of a work-experience course. She could have taken Lunar Catering or any one of a number of interesting options – Anton P'ntarr spent *his* two days servicing a deep-sea agricultural robot – but no, she chose instead to come into this huge crystal ball, a place flooded with light, where the trustees had assembled a collection of life forms from the nearer planets. Ugly things, most of them, but their foul habits and vile perfumes were not enough to keep Anton P'ntarr away. He came here often to observe his beauty among the beasts.

And today was rather a special day, for he had resolved to approach her, and speak to her, and let her know that he existed. He stood beside the transparent pen where they kept the Wheebler from the planet Dracena.

Oh beating heart be still! He spoke his first words to her.

"That's a very fine Wheebler you've got there."

"Yes, isn't it gorgeous," she said.

No, Anton P'ntarr did not find it gorgeous. Frankly, the thing was revolting from all angles. The Wheebler resembled a large lump of dough and possessed the power to deliver an electric shock of 1,000 volts. It could, besides, turn itself into any shape or form – or even, when in the mood, turn itself inside out.

"They begin life as a vegetable, you know," she said. "They're really one of the miracles of the Universe."

"I can easily believe it," replied Anton P'ntarr.

He wanted to tell her that she, too, was one of the

50

miracles of the Universe. She wore her shining hair piled high on her head in the latest fashion – it rose fully half a metre into the air, the various strands of it being held in place by a lattice of light wire. Careful girls kept this hidden, of course. Also, round the rims of her ears, she wore coils of dull gold. Anton P'ntarr knew that he had been guilty of staring and cleared his throat for the little speech he had prepared.

"Perhaps I should say who I am. My name is Anton P'ntarr and I'm in your compulsory Ecology classes at school."

"Oh, they're so boring, aren't they?"

"They are indeed. I'm hoping to be a dentist myself."

She pushed some food pills through the tiny holes in the Wheebler's pen, and the mouldy great lump heaved itself about in excitement.

"A dentist," she said, "isn't that a bit old-fashioned? I can't imagine anybody actually *choosing* to be a dentist in this day and age."

The silly girl seemed unaware of the fact that the human race has always relied rather heavily on its teeth. "Teeth are important," said Anton P'ntarr, but gently. He didn't want an argument. "You shouldn't overlook the cultural persistence of the white smile."

She smiled at him. "The cultural persistence of the . . . what? The white smile? That doesn't mean anything, it's just nonsense."

It probably was, but it didn't much matter; she was talking to him. He walked with her to the area reserved for the Whooping Primates of Cedonia.

"No, it's not. We *could* have red, green and orange teeth, the multi-coloured smile is perfectly feasible nowadays. But do people want it? They do not. Your white smile is here to stay and so are dentists."

She looked at him out of two of nature's perfect gems, illuminated merrily from within by her natural radiance. Anton P'ntarr hoped that he would not get carried away and say something stupidly romantic.

"Are you wise or have you a chromosome loose?" she asked him.

"Please tell me your name."

"What do you want my name for?"

"So that I can say it to myself, over and over again."

"You are missing a chromosome," she said, flicking open a gate labelled Authorized Personnel Only. The Whooping Primates had recognized her by now and had taken to screaming for their bellies to be filled. It was a rather desperate Anton P'ntarr who shouted after her, "Well then, can I call you on the Visiphone?"

"Excuse me," she replied, "I have to feed the Whooping Primates of Cedonia."

Nuts, nuts and more nuts to the Whooping Primates of Cedonia, thought Anton P'ntarr as he walked home across the roofs of the city; and he suffered every step of the way from the pangs of unrequited love. Really, it was quite pathetic what she had reduced him to. And without knowing it! She didn't know how powerful she was. He even felt jealous of the revolting Wheebler from the planet Dracena because she thought it was gorgeous. And if that didn't make him the biggest twit in the city.

Thoughts like these kept him busy until he reached home.

Anton P'ntarr lived with his father, his mother, his two brothers and little sister Leena in one of the fashionable Troglodyte Dwellings on the fringes of Ule.
These Troglodyte Dwellings were actually holes in the chalk hillside – caves. In the distant past, they had probably been inhabited by primitive people, advanced cousins of the Whooping Primates of Cedonia; millions of years later they had become a status symbol and the best thing you could say to social climbers like yourself was that you had "Just moved, you know, into one of the Troglodyte Dwellings." Anton P'ntarr's mother had warned all her children never, *never* to refer to their home as a cave, especially not in company. His mother was a dedicated snob, but he was fond of her just the same.

When he returned home to his cave that evening, he found the whole family assembled in one room; and quite clearly, something had excited them.

"Guess what!" little sister Leena yelled after plonking a smacker of a kiss on his nose. "Guess Anton, guess oh guess!" "Can't," said Anton P'ntarr, who was in no mood for silly games.

He noticed his mother's eyes. Shining, they were, in the failing light.

"Well? Isn't anybody going to tell me?" he inquired.

"Anton. Oh Anton," said his mother, "we finally got six Permits, my dear. We're all going on a time sleep. For a hundred and fifty years. Isn't it wonderful?"

That heart of his which had taken such a pounding this day began to act up again.

"A time sleep!" he managed to splutter.

His father held up six small, metal discs, rarer than gold dust. Their Permits to travel – you couldn't go without one. "The whole family!" said Father P'ntarr, and little Leena danced about on tiny bare feet, chanting,

We're going to be frozen, clap hands.

We're going to be frozen, clap hands.

Frozen. The popular, if erroneous term for human hibernation. All six of them would be put into cold storage and wakened up at some future date to savour the flavour of life in another time. You could 'Travel On' for 200 years, 150 years, or for 99 years and a day – whichever took your fancy. "Isn't it exciting," he heard his mother exclaim. "Think how different the world will be in the century after next, can you *imagine?*" And they all started talking at once, as if they were discussing some inconsequential thing like the prospect of a family holiday on the moons of Tyre.

Said Anton P'ntarr: "I'm not going."

He certainly was not. He could see no point whatever in breaking off the perfectly successful life he was enjoying in the here and now, in order to take it up again at some notional time in the future. Definitely not. He told them again, "You can throw my Permit away. I'm not going."

"Oh Anton!" said his mother. "You always were a stubborn child."

Inevitably, a row occurred. He got it hot and heavy from all sides. First they threatened him. They said they would get a Compulsory Order and *make* him come with them, but he calmly pointed out that he was too old by a matter of a few weeks

54

for a Compulsory Order to be binding on him. Then they wheedled. Think of all the sacrifices made for you, they said, and you won't even agree to come into the future with us. Oh Anton, *why* won't you come into the future with us? It's the perfect way to escape from the ruts and routines of life in the metropolis.

"I'm not in a rut," said Anton.

But you will be, they said. And you'll never get another chance, each person gets only one Permit, only one. Tens of thousands of people are scheming and bribing to get Permits, they said, it's such an *honour* to be selected for goodness sake. Only the best people are chosen for 'Travelling On', no convicts or degenerates are sent forward, none of your rabble. "The cream of society," said his mother, as if this was the most irrefutable argument of all, "only the very *cream.*"

"I'm staying put," said Anton P'ntarr.

After a day like that was it any wonder he had a dream?

The revolting Wheebler escaped from its pen and got among the General Public. There were horrendous scenes. People were trampled underfoot and others fainted clean away from fright as the thing turned itself into a long worm three or four kilometres long and surrounded the Ecology Building. But help was at hand. To the astonishment of all who were privileged to be there that day, Anton P'ntarr donned rubber gloves and rolled it up like a piece of hosepipe and returned the Wheebler to the trustees of the Inner-Space Menagerie. They were so delighted that they made him an honorary member of staff and he was able to see what's-er-name every day.

He woke up in a sweat, quivering with fear at the thought of what he'd just done. He might have had 1,000 volts up his arm and been fried to a frazzle. "If today is like yesterday," Anton P'ntarr promised himself, "I shall not get up tomorrow."

He took a decision. He quickly jumped out of bed and punched her Central Registration Number into the Visiphone before he lost his nerve. And suddenly there she was, glaring out at him from the screen on his wall.

She didn't look pleased.

"It's you. You've no business calling me at this time of the morning. I'm not fit to be seen."

No doubt about that. The lattice of light wire was still very apparent under her hair. Clearly she had not yet finished her toilette.

"I don't care what you look like," said Anton P'ntarr, "I love you."

"Don't be so silly, you hardly know me."

"Tell me your name."

"If you must know, it's Elena Mede Shahadnazar. My friends call me Mede."

Not a bit of wonder, he thought. Elena Mede Sha . . . Shazahad . . . "Can I call you Mede, too?"

"Well you can if you like. You don't have to get elected to a secret society to call me Mede. I'm a very ordinary person."

Ordinary! She didn't know, she had no idea.

"Not to me. You're a goddess to me."

"Is that a fact. Which one?"

He couldn't come up with the name of a goddess quickly enough, so he changed the subject.

"Will I see you in school? Are you going to compulsory Ecology at the end of the week?"

"Yes, worse luck."

"Meet me on the roof during break. Please. I'll protect you from the Waps and Wazza-wazzas."

That made her grin a little. She sat examining the cuticles of her fingernails, keeping him waiting for an answer.

"All right," she said, "I'll meet you on the roof."

The screen went blank, but it made no difference – he could still see her sitting there, putting the finishing touches to that impossible hair-do. Mede, he said. Mede, what a lovely name, Mede and Mede and Mede. And Mede and Mede and more Mede.

He had a thought on the way to school that morning. Maybe he should tell his parents about her, then they wouldn't keep at him to go disappearing off into the future. Imagine! He could waken up in the century after next madly in love with somebody who'd already been dead a hundred years. Surely they must see that *they* were the unreasonable party in this dispute, and not him.

Philosophical thoughts such as these slowed him down, naturally enough, so that he was late for school. His personal computer – they all had one – waited patiently for him with a message, "Student to be Warned," it whispered. Anton P'ntarr hit the registration key to show that he was present, and snarled, "Satisfied?" The face of the teacher appeared on the computer screen, the lights were dimmed and morning lectures commenced. Like the other thousand-odd pupils in the theatre, Anton P'ntarr heard why life died out on boring old planets like Earth and Ithica Three. And he wondered which lucky beast was being fed by Elena Mede Shazna . . . Shanaz . . . whatever – down at the Inner-Space Menagerie.

That same afternoon the six members of the P'ntarr family travelled by Zoomtube to the centre of the city, where they disembarked and climbed the worn, old, sandstone steps of one of the most historic and imposing buildings in the city of Ule.

This was the Institute of Longevity. They were on their way to get measured up for their travelling caskets and to receive the first of their anti-dream injections – except for Anton P'ntarr, who accompanied them merely in the role of observer. He still wasn't going.

At the entrance to the Institute, Father P'ntarr made them stop to marvel once again at one of the magnificent sights of the metropolis – the door. It towered above them at least thirty metres high, and in its entirety constituted the largest wooden artefact to have survived from the ancient civilizations of Clemess Amara. Into the centre of the door, on a raised boss, some anonymous craftsmen had carved a beautifully wrought and lifesize representation of the mythological Hoth staring into his crib. Little Leena recognized the look of agony on his face:

"Oh look, mummy, we've got that man in our house."

So they had. A cheap ornament of Hoth sat in an alcove near the window. Mother P'ntarr took her daughter firmly by the hand.

"Come along dear. And don't say 'house'. We live in a Troglodyte Dwelling."

The P'ntarrs walked the length of the Institute's central hall, the roof of which was carried high on slim colonnades of red, unpolished stone. The architects of this place – so it seemed to Anton P'ntarr – had been motivated by a desire to make human beings feel small. Every little sound they made returned to them with interest, like a reproach. Mother P'ntarr was busy saying "Shhh!" to nobody in particular, when suddenly an official-looking gentleman stepped out from behind a pillar and startled them all.

"The P'ntarr family, I presume?"

"Correct, Sir," said Father P'ntarr, never one to lose his composure for long, "we are here in our entirety."

"Hmm. This way please, we like to do our measuring in the Time Terminal."

He had a mincing sort of voice, this official gentleman, and a tendency to rub his hands together under his chin. He led them through to a place where a sign said:

TIME TERMINAL:

THIS ESTABLISHMENT IS DEDICATED

TO THE CONQUEST OF MANKIND'S

MOST DOGGED PURSUER, THE CHANGELING DEATH.

Several caskets were prominently displayed on a slowly-revolving stand. These caskets, about two metres long, appeared to be made of metal. Father P'ntarr did as the official gentleman said and climbed rather bashfully into one of the turning caskets to try it out. It had a purple lining. Watching his father travelling slowly round in circles, Anton P'ntarr thought that he had never in his life seen anything so daft.

"All you need is a pair of oars, dad. You could row into the future."

"Anton!" said his mother.

She felt the purple lining between finger and thumb.

"It also comes in pink or blue, Madam. The

casket itself is our very best alloy. Note the pseudo-brass handles for easy lifting – ornamental but useful like all the best art. You'll just *love* this casket, Sir."

Father P'ntarr waited until the revolving stand brought him back to his family. Raising his head from a horizontal position, he said, "I must say it feels rather comfortable."

"That lining, Madam. Real silk."

"Really?"

"Oh yes! Real natural fibre. You'll just love waking up in this, Madam."

"How do *you* know," grunted Anton P'ntarr, "you'll not be there to see her get up."

"Anton!" his mother rebuked him, "that's enough. Just because you've decided not to go, there's no need to mock." By way of explanation she added to the official, "He says he's in love."

"Huh!" said the official, as if all was now clear.

Now he took a computer from his pocket and recorded details about each member of the travelling party so that people would know a little about them when the time came to thaw them out in the century after next. Finally, he coughed and addressed Mother P'ntarr on a delicate matter.

"Does Madam have a choice of travelling garment?"

"Oh . . . I thought . . . I have a very pretty blue nightdress."

"Oh very tasteful, *most* appropriate."

"It would go with the blue lining."

"It absolutely would. May I quietly recommend a little rouge for the long sleep? After one or two hundred years one is apt to waken up a little . . . you know . . . a little wan."

60

But would she come, he wondered?

All the week he had that question at the back of his mind: Would his Elena Mede keep that promise to meet him on the roof of the Ecology Building? After a morning's study of fossils of cycads and ferns and petrified ammonites he escaped at last to the heights of the city and saw her waiting for him among the exotic blooms. The roofs of Ule were famous for their flowers. Seeds, gathered by interstellar spacecraft from the planets of the Semule Plain, had been planted all over the place with incredible profusion, so that every insect now thought of this fragrant corner of the world as Paradise. Waps and Wazza-wazzas buzzed round the head of Elena Mede Shaznawhatever – the fairest flower of all. A wind had got up, and because of her kite-like hairstyle, which was an affront to common sense, she came towards him listing.

"Well," she said, "fancy keeping a goddess waiting."

He felt really quite shy. As they began to walk it occurred to him that there was one brute of a problem about being so mightily under some other person's spell: you felt so *unworthy* when you were with her. Fortunately an enormous Wap began to orbit her head. Anton P'ntarr reached across and annihilated it. Splat!

"How are the animals?" he asked.

"Oh, fine."

"What do the Whooping Primates think of your hair?"

"I didn't ask them."

"Best not to."

She flung a critical glance in his direction. "I didn't come up here to be insulted, so be careful."

"I'm not insulting you. I've been saying your name all morning. Mede, Mede, Mede. Please – come Layering with me."

Layering: the perfect sport for lovers since it provided plenty of opportunities for physical contact if people wanted it – and of course, most people did. While Mede considered her answer, Anton P'ntarr looked away across the roofs of the city to where the sun picked out the spindly minarets of the Institute of Longevity. Not much to cheer him up in that direction. A few weeks more and his parents would be stretched out stiffer than a couple of icicles.

Said Elena Mede Shahadnazar: "All right. I'll come."

Perhaps all lovers are deeply pessimistic at the beginning of a romance. Certainly Anton P'ntarr could hardly trust his ears.

"You will?"

"Yes I will."

"You'll come Layering with me?" He annihilated a hugely buzzing Wazza-wazza in celebration. "Oh Mede, my darling Mede." And he seized her hand, and began to gobble it.

She said, "Come on, stop that when people are looking. I'll come Layering with you, but I don't want any funny business when we get into the Bubble, is that fair enough, Anton?"

"Oh absolutely," said Anton, like one who had never heard of funny business.

"And stop slaughtering insects. Even Wazza-wazzas have a role to play in the ecological pyramid of life."

Their relationship prospered. Even his mother

stopped saying things like, "Really, Anton, if you would just give yourself a good shake and get her out of your system," and accepted the fact that her eldest son had found a powerful, an overriding motive for staying in the present time.

Besides, he was quite right. He was just a couple of months too old for them to get a Compulsory Order.

Oh, but there were tears, of course, and tantrums as the inevitable day approached when the family would be split for ever. Anton went with them to the Institute of Longevity, and, to please his mother, accompanied them into the Time Terminal for a session of last goodbyes.

His father took his hand firmly, and whispered quietly that one could be certain of nothing in this life.

"Listen son, I really must say this to you. Affairs of the heart are notoriously fickle."

"I know that, dad."

"You're embarrassed, of course," said his dad, turning red, "but if you *do* want to come after us . . ."

Anton P'ntarr shook his head. Not again! "I won't."

"Fair enough. Just remember to look in Hoth's Crib."

"Good luck in the future, dad," said Anton P'ntarr.

His mother wailed that she would never see his grandchildren.

"Take pictures of them Anton, won't you? We'd like to see them before they die."

Yes, yes, of course he would leave film for them to see. And he kissed them one by one.

"I'll be famous by the time you lot wake up," he said cheerfully, adding to Leena, "you'll be learning about me in your History classes. That'll be a laugh."

He stayed until they received the last of their anti-dream injections, then left them to get on with their long sleep.

The swamps at Doonacre.

A deadly wasteland. From this area beyond the boundaries of the city, hissing clouds of crimson, white and pale-grey gases rose hundreds of metres into the air. Nothing ventured through Doonacre, neither on foot nor on the wing. And yet, from a long way off Doonacre you could see large, transparent bubbles rising and falling at different speeds through the colourful miasma. To the untrained eye they looked like uncommonly fragile and beautiful natural phenomena: in fact these were man-made Bubbles, and they had people in them, for this was the latest craze in entertainment for the citizens of Ule. One moment you went rolling down the dips caused by different densities of gas; the next you were flattened against the curved wall of your Bubble, on your way with a whoosh! to yet another pinnacle of pressure. On their rest days, Anton and Mede went Layering, as a rule.

They found it exciting to tempt fate by tumbling through layers of noxious gas in a Bubble of Oxygen – and it was private, too, way up there in the shifting, vivid sky: the perfect place, in fact, for young people who wanted a bit of slap and tickle with their rough and tumble. On one of their Layering days – it was to be their last, in fact –

Anton P'ntarr said to his Elena Mede, "I'll tell you something. You and I could make the most beautiful children."

She didn't answer, so he continued cheerfully, "I could look after their teeth and you could tell them stories about the bunch of horrors down at the Inner-Space Menagerie. Any new beasties?"

She sat staring out through the wall of the Bubble at another couple drifting by in an upward direction. They were locked in a clinch and clearly using up their oxygen at a fearful rate.

"Disgraceful," said Anton P'ntarr.

"Yes," said Mede, "we received a Malasander Bird from Colon Four. They live inside the rims of volcanoes."

"Beats a Troglodyte Dwelling any day."

"The Malasander Male vomits up its food to impress its mate; it's a fascinating courtship display. Glands in the throat sac turn the contents of the stomach bright green."

Yuk. Anton P'ntarr did not intend to be outdone by the Malasander Male from Colon Four. He told her his dream, the one about the Wheebler escaping, and explained how he had risked 1,000 volts to capture it in a feat of courage which astonished the General Public. And all for the love of Elena Mede Sha . . . Shaznadahar . . . ?

"Well, I know," he finished modestly, "that it doesn't compare with bright green *vomit*, but you've got to admit I'm trying."

"Oh," she suddenly declared with a rush, "I do love you, Anton P'ntarr."

But she was sitting there with tears in her eyes. He straightened her up with a hand on either shoulder.

"Mede. What's wrong with you today?"

"I'm sorry," she said, composing herself, "I've really been quite brave about it until now. Mind you, they only told me yesterday." And she sniffed, before adding bitterly, "We've been selected."

"What for?"

"Anton, you can *guess* what for."

He stood up in the Bubble until his head hit the tough, rubbery circumference. Of course he could guess, it was happening to him again.

"But you can refuse to go!" he shouted.

She shook her head in misery.

"Can't. I can't, Anton. They've taken out a Compulsory Order for me. I have to go."

Their Bubble was sinking with a soft hiss through a scarlet cloud with a foaming black heart. What brutal people parents could be, he was thinking, when they really put their minds to it. He asked her an academic question, "How long?"

"Oh Anton. Ninety-nine years and a day."

And away she went from him, 'Travelling On' without moving a muscle, leaving him a prisoner in the present time, and pining for her as if he were one of the uglies down at the Inner-Space Menagerie.

Anton P'ntarr had grown up in a city to which there were two tiers. Over the centuries, the roofs of Ule had gradually evolved into a vast precinct for the exclusive use of pedestrians. Hundreds of narrow bridges – from the ground they seemed marvellously delicate things, like the work of spinning insects – linked each roof to the next in an ongoing promenade of gardens, observatories, blue lakes and numerous other amenities. There were seven hundred such bridges in Ule. In the days following the departure of his Elena Mede, Anton P'ntarr walked every one of them. He had the air about him of one whose spirit has taken leave of the body, and flown.

Ninety-nine years and a day. Well, they might as well let her sleep for one day short of never, for all it mattered now.

Oh yes, he thought bitterly, he might see her again. People could expect to cheat the Changeling for a hundred and twenty years and more if they looked after themselves. He'd be a hundred and fifteen years old when she woke up. He could see himself an old man with a beard down to his toes, standing in an unobtrusive place in the Time Terminal, watching her emerge so fresh, so young, still beautiful, his unattainable, lovely Mede.

Would she look round? Would she remember and look round for him, just in case? Oh! to have his Permit, to sleep and be wakened the day before her and to raise her from the vulgar purple lining with a kiss! Ye gods, ye gods, he was thinking, what cruel blows Mankind is made to bear.

He caught sight of old Hoth up there in the southern sky, bent over his Crib, a face on him as if he was the daddy of all misery. *He* knew. Poor old Hoth, poor old Anton P'ntarr, two of a kind.

Hoth's Crib . . . ?

He began to walk quickly, feet keeping pace with his mind, something his father had said about Hoth's Crib . . .

But what? It had all been rather emotional and embarrassing, their last chats together, all temper and no sense, he hadn't taken any of it in. Until now.

O ye gods – until now! Suddenly his feet wouldn't be content with just walking, mere walking wouldn't do. His feet began to run, his lungs began to ache, his mind soared.

In the Troglodyte Dwelling he paused, breathless, staring up at the cheap representation of Hoth and warning himself that perhaps, after all, he was wrong. Surely his father had thrown the Permit away. Anton P'ntarr had told him to do that often enough.

With reverent hands he lifted down the ornament – here was an object which had presided over his childhood and given him dreams. He looked into the crib. In the hood which traditionally hid the Changeling's face from human eyes, he saw a bright little disc.

His ticket to ride for ninety-nine years and a day.

Sam McBratney: "It's nice to write and to read 'true to life' stories. The situations in them are familiar and the people seem 'real'.

There's another kind of story. I'm thinking of the Round Table, Cuchulainn, Gulliver, Alice, and of the Ugly Duckling and thousands of other characters who are, shall we say, a little bit larger than life. There have always been story-tellers who make it their business to take us beyond the known world into the fantastic, and to charm us with tales of wonder.

Science has been telling us that there is a Universe out there. They say it may be empty but story-tellers who love the fantastic can't leave it alone. They are busy trying to fill it with the contents of their imaginations. And it's free! Go on . . . have a go."

SUDDENLY THERE CAME A CRACK IN THE ICE

Petronella Breinburg

(A story set in the Hague)

"You? You of all people!"

The words came back to Cita as if from the cold wind blowing against her face. She pulled her woolly hat closer over her ears. The hat in itself seemed to be a symbol of defiance. "Teachers," she laughed. "They hate anyone who wears such a hat which displays the colours of the new Surinamse flag." Cita was right. Girls, and boys too, had more than once been told by their teachers to "take that ridiculous thing off your head". That is, the Creoles got told off. They were the ones brave enough to wear them. Cita, like the other Hindustani girls from Surinam, liked the colours, but was afraid to wear one.

"Funny," Teneke had more than once laughed, "how people could hate a simple hat."

Teneke was Cita's best friend in those days. Now it was Teneke who had got her into trouble. If it wasn't for Teneke, none of this would have happened. Cita felt sure that it was Teneke who went and told Mr Van Oost, the teacher on break-duty, that Cita was speaking Surinams. The teacher came and caught Cita. Maybe if she had stopped speaking, the teacher would have just given her a warning cough or clearing of his throat.

For an unexplained reason, Cita did not stop. She continued to explain the maths homework to a young third year, in Hindustani. The girl was new, from the special-class where all foreign pupils went before they were transferred to the general class. She was terribly nervous and unsure of herself. Because of that nervousness, Cita felt sure, the girl could not do the work. The girl was getting very low marks, so the tutor told her off, and this made her more nervous and caused her to make more mistakes.

That day Cita had found the girl in tears in the girls' toilet. She managed to speak to her and bring her back to the homework room. Cita had begun to explain in Dutch, but the girl didn't seem to understand the problem, and continued to sniff. It was then that Cita broke one of the most important rules of the school, the rule that said none of the Surinam languages were permitted in school. People who broke that rule were severely punished. They had to stay in after school and do their Dutch homework, of if they were behind in French or German, they were allowed to do extra work in those subjects.

"Damned unfair." Cita stamped in the ice. It had been snowing again and the Zuider Park, near the school, was high with soft ice in places.

"It's like sugar, lots and lots of white sugar." Cita began to run along the ice, kicking sprays of it into the air.

That action brought back to her mind the first day she met Johan. If it wasn't for Johan, she and

Teneke would have still been best friends. Teneke would not have told on her. Cita would not have been called to the tutor's office, and she would not have been told off and told to report for staying in after school. And she would not have refused to take punishment for speaking her own language. And she would not have been given a choice.

"Either you take your punishment or you take suspension. You know the rules." Cita pursed her lips to imitate the tutor.

"Bloody scarecrow she is," Cita swore under her breath, then automatically looked round to see if anyone had heard her. Because, brave as she was only an hour ago, she still could never swear for anyone to hear.

"Crunch, crunch," the hardening ice said under her feet.

"It's like walking on broken glass," she smiled in spite of her sadness.

How Cita liked the crunching of half-hard ice when she first arrived in Holland from Surinam, exactly five years before. She had arrived in seventy-seven and now it was eighty-two. She liked Holland then and still would like it now. "If only the school didn't have those silly rules," she thought. "Why can't the Surinam children speak Surinams when the Moroccan children and the English children are all allowed to speak their mother tongue. Not fair, not bloody fair, and I don't care if I am suspended! Don't care one damn!"

Cita's thoughts were braver than she actually felt. What would she tell her father? "Dad will go berserk. He wants me to do well, and I *am* doing well. I got top marks in English, my German is brilliant – even that scarecrow with her giraffe neck said so. My French is not too bad, either. I must work harder on my French, that's all. Anyway, I was the first Surinam girl to move up from the school's low stream to a high stream, so I can't be bad. No Surinam girl ever got out of a low stream before. God, what am I going to tell my dad?

Maybe I should go back to school, go back and say I'm sorry. Other people have done it, why not me? Why can't I be like all the other girls and say I was sorry for speaking Hindustani? I've done it before, another time when I was caught speaking it?" Next moment Cita asked, "But why should I? That damn Teneke, damn her, damn Johan, damn the whole school, damn Holland! I'm fed up! Wish I was back in St Maria School in Paramaribo. There you don't have all these stupid rules. And you don't have people like that Teneke."

Cita had been jogging while thinking but had now got to stop. She had jogged a long way and was tired. She found herself a bench and sat down. "Oh, God, what am I going to do now? I can't go home and tell them I was suspended, I just can't. They'll kill me, they'll skin me alive . . . they . . ."

"Cita," a voice called loudly from behind her. That voice startled her. She knew that voice well. She had heard it for the first time, right here in that very park. She had heard it many times since. She had heard it at the local community centre where she and her brothers had gone to a festival of Hindustani art. She was surprised to find him admiring the exhibits because he was no Hindustani, he was Creole.

"What happened? Teneke said you got suspended and that you're blaming her. What *is* going on? You can't get suspended! Not you, you're the best girl in the school. The best girl in the whole of Den Hage even, you're, eh, my eh, special girl." He sat himself, uninvited, beside her.

"Don't talk nonsense, I'm not your girl, special or not special. Anyway, I *can* get suspended if I want to."

"No you can't! You'll go right back there and stay in school."

"Who are you to tell me what to do?" Suddenly Cita was angry. He looked so handsome that she had to be angry with him. If she wasn't angry with him she might love him. And if she loved him he might notice it. And if he noticed it he might want to see her more often. Teneke would go berserk, and when Teneke went berserk, the whole school shivered. Cita remembered the incidents when something had upset Teneke, making her scream and shout. Cita recalled her 'beating people up'.

"Look," he said, not looking at her. "I know how you feel. It is like the old days back home when our grandparents were beaten if they spoke Sranan."

"The Hindustanis were beaten too," she joined in.

"True, but did that stop Hindustani or Sranan? No, it didn't, not one bit it didn't. All the boys at my school speak Sranan or Hindustani. They even have a place in Amsterdam where you can learn to write in Sranan."

"What's that got to do with me here, that's what I want to know? Amsterdam is Amsterdam, maybe there the teachers are more, eh, civilized. Anyway, you'd better go." Cita got off the bench and pulled nervously at her woolly hat.

On one hand, his presence made her very uncomfortable. On the other hand, she wished he would stay. He was a nice boy. Why couldn't he stay and talk to her if he wished? "Teneke'll kill you if he does, that's why," the ice crunching beneath her feet seemed to say.

"You cold?" he asked.

"Of course I'm not." Yet she seemed to have goose pimples all over her.

"Look, go back to school. Take the punishment. Anyway, it is no punishment if it doesn't hurt. So don't let it hurt. Just do any homework they set you. You're clever anyway, you'll finish it in no time and go home. When you leave school, you'll go to Amsterdam and learn to write in your own language. Nobody can stop you then. Nobody can stop them speaking Dutch no matter where they live, so nobody can stop us."

"He speaks like a grown man. He sounds so clever," Cita thought, and wondered why he was sent to a technical school instead of a HAVO, which is a higher school. It was to HAVO that all the clever people went. "Everybody knows that 'technical school' is a nice name for 'dumb school'. He is no dumby, and he looks so handsome. He could be a president one day if he wanted to. He could be anything, God even, if he wanted to . . ."

"I know you're cold. I can tell. You're shivering."

"Well, I am a bit. I got so mad I came out without my coat."

"Take mine." He pulled off his coat and put it over her shoulders.

Side by side they continued to walk through the park. Occasionally she'd kick some soft ice. He too would kick some, and pretended that he could not kick further than she could. She knew he was pretending. He could kick much further than that.

He was pretending, to make her happy, and the thought that he wanted to make her happy, made her happy.

"Hi . . ." A long cry came and jerked Cita from her romantic dream. She looked round, but need not have done so. Somehow she knew that voice. It belonged to Teneke, Teneke Groen, who else?

"Oh, bloody hell! Where're they all going?" he said.

"Hi, you! I knew I'd find you here," said Teneke, and a group of about six girls, led by The Teneke, ran up to where Cita and Johan were.

Teneke puffed, so the other girls puffed as well. None of them would have dared not to puff if Teneke was puffing.

"We've (puff) got it all (puff) organized." Teneke took a deep breath.

"Yes, and Tien is our leader, aren't you?" a girl said. It was little Liesje. Poor Liesje who agreed with everything Teneke said, or got her face smashed in.

"Now, if *you* get suspended, we all take suspension. All the Surinam girls, don't know about the boys." Teneke gave Johan a dirty look. "And some of the Dutch girls too."

Cita was puzzled. Was Teneke saying that she was actually on her side? Cita wanted to say something more, but just managed a guttural, "What?"

"See, I told you!" Johan smiled. "You got supporters, I told you!"

"I am no footballer." Cita seemed to find her voice at last.

"Where is the paper? Who's got the damn paper?" Teneke said in coarse Sranan.

The two Dutch girls in the group could not, of

course, understand, so they looked vaguely at Teneke.

"Who's got the paper with the names?" Teneke repeated.

"Names, what names?" asked Cita.

"Come on ladies, you can't stand here chatting in the ice, that child is going to get in an accident there, the ice is cracking!" Johan pointed to children playing, but the group took no notice.

The group began to walk along while Teneke explained, to Cita's horror, that all the names on the list were of girls who said that they'd stand by Cita.

"You've got a right to speak your own language," said Marelijn. "My dad said so. He said, as long as you write in good Dutch you can speak Plat-Haagse if you want to. 'Let any teacher punish you for it, and I'll come to that school and break necks,' he said," Marelijn laughed.

"And he will too, I've seen him at his market stall," said Teneke.

"My dad can't break necks, you see." Cita felt better. If these girls could be on her side then all was well. She wouldn't even mind being punished.

"No, but if my dad and other parents . . ." Marelijn began, but Teneke stopped her.

"No parents, just us, right?" Teneke stared into Marelijn's blue eyes.

"Just us," all the girls, except for Cita, said in unison.

"Now, we'll sign a petition. Telma, you're doing typing, you type out the words . . . 'We the girls of . . .' Oh, who's best at Dutch? Who should write it."

"That would be Anne. She's top at Dutch," said someone.

"Yes, I will," said Anne.

"What are you grinning for?" Teneke asked Johan.

Cita had, for the moment, forgotten Johan's presence.

"And don't you, Cita, go telling people I got you in trouble, and because of him. I did not for one thing, and for him? You must be joking. She can have him, can't she girls?"

"Oh, yes, she can," the girls chorused.

"But now we must plan. Tomorrow, you, Cita, you come to school as usual. You say sorry to the old scarecrow. Of course, you wouldn't call her scarecrow to her face. You must be all nice and stupid, and say, well, blame it on . . ." Teneke whispered to Cita. "Say it's your menstrual, your . . ."

"Sh!" Cita pushed Teneke away and blushed, even though she was sure that from where Johan was standing he could not have overheard.

"Then we'll start the petition rolling." Teneke continued to give orders. "We'll need . . . Hi, Helen, your dad's photocopier's working again, is it?"

"Yes, I can make one for each of us six. Eh, five assistant leaders take a copy round to the whole school and you keep a copy," Helen said.

"What about other schools?" asked Anne.

"Ladies, may a mere boy speak?" Johan mocked.

"Yes, you may." Teneke gave permission before Cita had a chance to open her mouth.

"The boys at my place, can they sign as well?" asked Johan.

"I'm not going to go round asking boys," said Cita.

"I can do it," said Johan.

"But you're not at our school," reminded Helen.

"His girl is, so he can help," said Teneke.

"I'm, eh, not his girl, eh," Cita stammered.

"Of course you are, liar! We'll give him a copy to take to his place. I say so. Now, let's get to our houses, leave these two love birds."

With that Teneke and the girls went as suddenly as they came, waving.

"Strange girl that Teneke. She makes me, well, I can't speak when she's around. And I thought she was, well, your girl."

"Nah, she's got another boy, thank God. She was beginning to get on my nerves with her bullying. She's turned her attention to Ronald."

"Poor Ronald. Anyway, I must go home now."

"And you are my girl, aren't you? I can only take the petition around if you are."

Cita wanted to speak but it was as if something held on to her tongue, and unless you move your tongue, you cannot speak.

She did not speak for a long time while they walked side by side, until he said, "The ice is beginning to melt. See over there."

"Ja, that child had better be careful staying on that pond."

"Ja, it's beginning to crack," said Johan.

For Cita, it was as if a very new beginning was following the end of an era. She pulled her woolly hat back into place to cover her ears, "I'm going to school tomorrow, and won't let that Teneke do all the talking, either!"

"Good, I'll wait for you in the playground, no matter how long your punishment homework, OK?"

"Yes, wait for me."

Petronella Breinburg was born in Surinam, South America, where the population is multi-ethnic and multi-lingual with Dutch as the language of education. She has taught for many years in South America and the United Kingdom, and has travelled widely in Europe. A large number of her books for young people are available in Swedish, Danish, Norwegian, Dutch and Portuguese. This story is based on her research in inner city schools in Holland through which she has found that, as in the old colonial days, Surinam children are forbidden to speak their <u>own</u> language even though they are encouraged to learn German, French, English and even Latin. Petronella has found many Citas, Johans and Tenekes.

FLYING DUSTBINS
David Rees

Miss Lindley, everyone knew, couldn't keep order. Old Spindly Lindley! Her lessons were chaos. Nobody learned anything; pellets were flicked; ink was spilled; paper darts flew round the room. "Spindly! Lindley! Longnose!" The familiar words came over the hubbub of kids milling about in the playground. She turned. There was a sea of faces grinning and giggling at her. She picked on Allan. "Me, Miss? I never said a thing!" He looked angry. They stared at each other; Miss Lindley gave in first. "Was it you, Ivor?" The bell rang, and her question was lost in the surge of children pushing into the school. Simon found himself carried by the tide of shoving arms and legs; he was pressed up against Allan, his cousin. "Don't push me, Emerson!" Allan shouted and dug Simon with his elbow.

Why did his cousin have to be so unpleasant? Simon couldn't understand it. After all, Allan's family seemed to have all the luck. They hadn't been bombed out as he had. Their house hadn't even lost a slate! Simon remembered when four incendiary bombs had dropped on Aunt Mary's garden. The leaves of the plum tree had been charred and the cabbages burned. One bomb, it was true, had pierced the garage roof, and if Uncle Ben's car had been there, things could have been nasty. But it wasn't; the bomb smouldered away quietly and burned itself out: no one discovered it for a week. Yet the fuss Aunt Mary made!

In Room Five the Third Years waited for Miss Lindley. As usual there was a tremendous noise, and, as usual, Miss Lindley was late: she didn't dare face them until the last possible moment. Allan was at the door. "She's coming!"

"Right, start again, Susan."

They were quieter while Susan, a small, fair girl with a serious-looking face, spelled the word 'cataclysm'. They were hoping she would make a mistake. "Now 'mantelpiece', Susan. Stand up straight."

"I am standing up straight." There were grins at this. Susan was a mouse of a girl and there was no other teacher she would have dared to answer back.

"Go on."

"M-a-n-t- Ow! Miss . . . Allan pinched me."

"Ooooh!" Allan, who sat behind, was on his feet. "The whopping liar! I never touched her!" He was outraged. "Say that again and I *will* pinch you!"

"That's enough, Allan! Go on, Susan, M-a-n-t-. What's next?"

"I never heard the like!" Allan said. "Did you, Ivor? I —" There was a chorus of agreement, supporting Allan.

"Right!" shouted Miss Lindley. "Everybody spell it. All together."

"M-a-n-t-e-l-p-i-e-c-e!!" The headmaster's study was next door. He was meeting children who would be new First Years next September, and their parents. "I don't want to be disturbed this morning," he had said to the assembled teachers in the staff room, looking pointedly at Miss Lindley.

"Ssssh, ssssh!" she said, and they all replied "SSSSSSH!!!" Then they started to laugh, and someone called out "Spindly! Lindley! Longnose!"

"Please, Miss, how do you spell 'spindle'?" That was Ivor, dark-eyed and mischievous, the cheekiest of them all. Another burst of laughter greeted this; he grinned at his friends, enjoying their approval.

The door opened. "Can I see you for a moment, Miss Lindley?" It was the headmaster, Mr Enever.

Yvonne was staring at her with a look of contempt; Richard was openly laughing at her. Juliet, as usual, was wandering round the room; Amanda was fighting Rodney; Neil was banging Robert on the head with a book; Jill and Janet were licking each other's tongues. Mr Enever noted it all. Simon watched, his eyes angrily taking in every detail. Out in the corridor a portly woman in a large hat looked in at the scene, horrified.

Miss Lindley went out and the door shut. Immediately everyone started discussing the lesson they had just wrecked; what a stupid lesson it was! Serve her right if she got sacked! She was only trying to copy Miss Bond, Allan said. Miss Bond was an old ruin of a woman to look at, but she certainly knew how to control them. They never even dared to whisper in her classes.

"Don't you think Simon Emerson is like Spindly Lindley?" said Allan. "All thin and soppy and wet.

83

Thirteen! He looks more like a ten-year-old!"

The class laughed. "Take a look in the mirror," Simon shouted. He flushed with anger.

"Take a look in the mirror," Ivor mimicked. "It'd crack when you looked in it!"

"Oh dear, what a calamity," Richard sang. "Simon's made a mess in the lavatory!" There was more laughter and other voices joined in the singing. It swelled to a loud chorus. Simon banged with rage on his desk, but it only encouraged them the more. He stood on his chair and kicked his feet against the wall – he hadn't the courage to kick another person – and screamed.

The door opened. "Get down, Simon! How dare you!" It was Miss Lindley.

"Please, Miss, have you just been sacked?"

This was the most daring remark Ivor had ever made, and he was rewarded with a sudden silence, and a gasp from Juliet. Miss Lindley stepped towards him, her hands open, as if she would grip him by the neck and throttle him. She stopped. "Open your *English Made Easy*," she said, in a high, strangled voice.

Simon seethed. He hated them, he hated them! One day he would hit out, kill them! He wouldn't stop like Lindley had done! He *loathed* being at school! How dare they . . .

"It must be true," said Rodney, the boy next to him.

"What?"

"She must have got the sack."

Simon hid behind a gate from the gang who all lived in Fernleaf Avenue: Allan, Ivor, Neil, Richard, Christine, Janet, Jill and Juliet – whom all the boys liked. They were listening to Neil as he explained something, demonstrating with his hands. They all tried to crowd together in a line across the pavement, but the girls were jostled out on to the grass verge. They were Miss Lindley's biggest headache, this group; they were bolder and ruder and cheated more than any of the other kids.

"... desk lids banging! Greatest we've done yet!" They all laughed as Neil finished. It had happened when Miss Lindley was trying to explain the plot of *Hamlet*; the front row was listening, and as the rest of the class was only talking quietly, she did not provoke them by shouting for complete silence. Then, at a pre-arranged signal, the desk lids were raised and one after the other they were all dropped in rapid succession. Mr Enever did not appear, even after the howls of laughter that followed, but Simon felt his eyes boring through the wall.

"Oh, but I like her," said Jill. "Don't you, Jan?"

"S'pose so." Janet shrugged.

"Like her!" said Allan. "You're batty."

"We can do what we want, can't we? Better than old Bondy."

There were murmurs of general agreement that she was better than old Bondy.

"But it's daft," said Ivor. "You don't learn anything, do you? What's the point?"

"Doesn't matter," said Allan. "Do it, Ju?"

"I think she's a cow," said Juliet. "I hate her."

"Why?"

"I just do."

"She can't help it, can she? I feel sorry for her."

They were well past, almost out of earshot. Simon turned and looked after them. They were squeezing through a hole in the cemetery railings.

He reached the shops. 'Fall of Rome', said a newspaper headline. 'General Mark Clark in Eternal City! Americans in Mussolini's capital!' Soon there would be the invasion: night after night just recently he had been woken by the drone of lorries; once he had slipped out of bed and lifted the corner of the curtain and seen their dimmed headlights, dozens of them, passing in convoys.

"It's D-Day!!" Richard was coming up the street waving a Union Jack.

"It's raining, it's raining; Hitler got a caning!" That was Janet and Jill, the inseparables.

Allan, several yards ahead, called out, "Don't be such babies!"

Simon was walking behind Miss Lindley. Juliet swirled past him and stopped by her. It was very odd; nobody ever talked to Miss Lindley if they could help it. Usually the kids either ignored her or giggled and dashed past, or said, "Good morning Miss Lindley," with exaggerated politeness, the boys lifting their caps right off their heads.

"Have you heard, Miss?" Juliet asked. Why are you speaking to her, Simon wondered. You called her a cow. "We'll be in Paris next week."

"The war will soon be over," said Miss Lindley, absurdly pleased that the girl had stopped to speak to her.

"We'll have all sorts of things we haven't dreamed of for years. Bananas. What do they taste like? I've forgotten."

Simon tried to imagine the taste, but it was so long ago he could not. The boys ahead were waiting. Juliet talking to Miss Lindley might seem peculiar to them, but it wouldn't stop them waiting for Juliet. Ivor and Allan fell in beside them.

"Why's it called D-Day, Miss?" Juliet asked. "What's the 'D' stand for?"

"Darling day," said Ivor, and Juliet blushed and giggled.

"I expect there are troops going ashore now," Miss Lindley said.

Simon pictured the invasion in his mind's eye, soldiers running into the sand dunes. Dunkirk in reverse, his mother had said. He plucked up courage and stepped into the conversation; he had something to say which he knew would interest them. "The Germans have a secret weapon that's going to blow us all to bits," he said.

Ivor spoiled it, however, for he, too, had heard this piece of information. "It's like a flying dustbin," he said. "And it doesn't have a pilot."

"Flying dustbin! What next!" They all shrieked with laughter.

"You're both fools," said Allan. Ivor started to punch him. Allan ran across the road and along the opposite pavement; Ivor followed.

"What does he mean, Miss, a flying dustbin?" Janet asked. "Is he right?"

"Of course not!" They walked on for a moment in silence: it was as if her remark had settled the problem.

"She's got the sack after all," Juliet whispered to Simon. "Mum heard somehow. It's a shame."

He was too overcome to reply. Juliet had actually spoken to him! To *him*!

"See, what did I tell you?" Ivor had run all the way to catch them up; he was panting. "They're pilotless planes. It says so in today's paper."

"They're not flying dustbins, anyhow," said Juliet. "I never heard anything so silly." Ivor, it seemed, already bored her.

"My Dad was firewatching on the Air Ministry roof. He saw the first one, and thought it was an ordinary plane. It flew up the river, through the searchlights, straight ahead. There were anti-aircraft guns going all round, but on it went. Dad said to himself 'That Jerry's got some courage –'" He stopped; Juliet was already talking to Allan.

"It's going to be very difficult for us all," said Miss Lindley. "There might even be another blitz." The early morning walk had now become part of the day's routine. Word had got round that Miss Lindley had been sacked: Juliet's mother told Christine's mother who told Neil's mother who told Neil's father, and the result was a long lecture on behaviour that Neil had been forced to listen to, on and off, for a whole evening. The children felt guilty. They'd enjoyed making their teacher's life a misery, but causing her to lose her job was not their intention. "We went too far," Juliet said, and the others agreed. So they began each day with a genuine show of friendliness, but something happened to them when they entered their classroom. Old habits were hard to change, and though the rudeness and cheek were perhaps not as bad as before, lessons continued to be chaotic.

"There won't be another blitz," said Allan. "The Germans are losing."

The air-raid warning sounded. They all looked at Miss Lindley.

"There's a shelter at the bottom of this road," she said. "Quick, but don't panic." Simon began to worry; wouldn't it have been better to dash on to school? They would certainly have got there in time. All this talk about pilotless planes was frightening; suppose something dreadful happened, and Miss Lindley didn't know what to do? Nine o'clock in the morning: it was a most unusual hour for an air-raid.

The shelter door had been left open and rain had flooded in during the night, but they slopped through it without protest. There was a dank, lived-in smell, and somewhere water dripped. There was a loud clang as Ivor kicked a tin; echoes magnified in there, and they jumped in surprise.

"I don't like it, Miss," said Juliet. "It's creepy!"

"I've never been in a public shelter before," Allan said.

There was a plane in the distance. They stopped talking – they had been saying how great it was not to be in Mr Enever's assembly – and listened. Was it a plane? It sounded like more than one plane, and yet not quite two. Simon tensed with fear; it was one of those pilotless horrors: he was sure of it. The noise increased. It was obvious now that it had only one engine, but it was not like any plane he had ever heard. It was more like a motor-bike.

"It sounds as if it's a Norton with a cracked exhaust-box," said Ivor in an awed whisper.

The noise stopped. Allan gripped Miss Lindley's arm and said "I'm frightened."

The explosion shook the shelter and they sagged sideways; for one terrifying second it seemed certain that the roof would fall on them. A house was collapsing; walls, ceilings, bedrooms tumbling with a roar like water, like rocks rolled in an immense cylinder. Little stones trickled; dust whirled in the shelter. There was light: the door had been blown off its hinges. Allan whimpered, still clutching Miss Lindley. The others sat frozen, wide-eyed with fear. .

"Stop it," Simon said. Allan stood up; his legs wobbled and he sat down again, hurriedly.

"Miss." It was Juliet. "You haven't been sacked, have you?"

After a moment Miss Lindley said, "No."

"Good." She sounded really pleased. "Good. Good!"

"Can we go?" asked Ivor. The all-clear was sounding.

They came out into the light. People were shouting and running; a woman was scrabbling frenziedly in the rubble of a wrecked house.

Allan sniffed, and dabbed his eyes with a handkerchief. Simon looked at him, then walked on with Juliet. It was a warm summer morning. Through the gap where the house had been they could see a garden with flowers in bloom.

"We mustn't be too late for school," said Miss Lindley. They set off, not realizing that Ivor had disappeared. He caught up with them and presented Miss Lindley with a bouquet of lupins.

"They're from that house," he explained. "Nobody would want them now."

"Ivor, that's . . . how kind!"

He looked embarrassed and the others laughed. Allan sniffed again. His eyes were dry now, but hot and swollen. Simon, on the other hand, felt elated. His class-mates had stopped persecuting him; Juliet actually seemed to like him; Allan would never again dare to be such a bully; and Miss Lindley was someone you could respect after all.

I don't hate school now, he said to himself.

David Rees: "This story is based on my memories of school at the end of the Second World War. There were some very strange teachers in those days, as many members of the permanent staff of schools had been called up to fight in the war."

THE RESCUE OF KAREN ARSCOTT
Gene Kemp

Amongst us lot she stuck out like a sore thumb. Or rather an orchid on a rubbish tip. Not that I know what an orchid looks like but you get the idea. She first appeared at our Wednesday morning Assembly, stuck there in line between Lindy Brown and Karen Arscott and there couldn't have been any place to do more for her – talk about a rose between two thorns. Lindy is knee high to a corgi, but thin with it, pipe cleaner shape, with a drippy nose and straggly hair. Her main hobby is weeping in corners. Mrs Conway, that's our class teacher, keeps leading us aside in turn, asking us to be *kind*, telling us to try to get her to join in. Poor Lindy had problems, she says, who doesn't, asks my friend Angie, rolling her big eyes.

Now Karen is different. Worse. Worse than anything you can imagine. She looks like that creature from the Black Lagoon, or out of the depths of the Id or whatever it was in those old movies. Get out of my way, she snarls. So I do. We all do. I've been getting out of her way for the past ten years since she flattened me in the Infants' playground and took my lunch and my new pencil case. Next day I brought my Mum into the playground. After she'd gone, Karen flattened me again. After that I gave up saying anything about Karen – just learnt to move very fast in the opposite direction whenever I saw her. And the boys learnt to move even faster. On one of her bad days she could clear the playground quicker than the school dentist arriving. When we left the Primary we hoped she'd go to a different Comprehensive. We kept saying all the good things we knew about the others very loudly when she was about. But it was hopeless, as we realized when we heard her Mom telling our teacher that Karen didn't want to leave her form mates. Her Mom looked like Giant Haystacks, the wrestler, so our teacher agreed, nodding up and down a lot.

But practice had made me very nippy, and there was a good crowd of us – Angie, Tamsin, Jackie and Pat. So we managed without too much aggro even when she turned up in our class despite there being four streams to each year.

No, the one who copped it all was Lindy, fresh from another school and a born loser from the start. We did try to stop it, to help, but Lindy was so wet and Karen so tough that by our year it was more or less the thing that those two paired off and Karen was The Boss.

And then, there in the hall one gloomy February morning stood this girl in between the two of them. And she was beautiful. Her hair was long and black, her face was pale, her eyes misty. Even Angie looked ordinary beside her. The rest of us like Rejects United.

Back in the classroom everyone crowded round

her as they always do with anyone new till the novelty wears off. I tried to join in but there was no room so I thought I might just as well get on with the homework I hadn't finished the night before. Then I made out a beauty programme wondering if Mum would let me dye my hair. It would be smashing not to be a natural born mouse, and to be slim. Not that I'm really very fat, and a thirty-six bra sounds all right except if you're only five foot tall you look more as if you're wearing a bolster than the Dawson Comprehensive answer to Miss World. Then I chucked the list away. Why bother? Never, never in a million light years was I going to look like that new girl. What was her name? Harriet, Mrs Conway was saying, Harriet Carter. Just look at Darren Carr making shapes with his hands in the air. He would, the cheeky so and so.

"Lisa, pay attention, please. Lisa!"

I sat up. "Yes Miss."

Back to basics.

She turned out to be a very quiet girl. Her work was good and she didn't put a foot wrong with the teachers or anyone, being friendly to everyone but not too friendly and going straight home after school. She seemed to live some distance away, no one knew where. In fact Harriet was a bit of a mystery, and rumours soon ran round the school that a) she was a South American millionairess in hiding because of kidnapping threats, b) she was a refugee from Eastern Europe, c) her mother was dead and she had to get home to cook for her Dad. Somehow the last seemed the most likely. So, said Angie, she's got problems, too.

In the end she just became another one of the

class. The boys gave up chasing her when they saw she really wasn't interested, and focus switched back to Angie who was now going out with the captain of the soccer team, who (they said) had never been out with a girl before. What will she make of him, we wondered. Also, we were doing a bit of work, since the teachers mostly came in saying, There's only so many weeks left now till the exams, filling us with terror – well some of us.

It was a very wet spring term. Every day it rained. Karen developed boils on her face which didn't do much for her looks and even less for her temper. Lindy actually appeared in new PE kit. Miss Johnson had gone on at her so much I suppose she was driven to it. Karen threw it down the loo so that it was soaking wet for the lesson. For once Lindy complained and for once we backed her, and Karen caught it in the neck, detentions for a week, etc. But Lindy appeared with a bruise on her face. Walked into a door she said quietly, my own silly fault, I ought to wear my glasses.

We stayed indoors at lunchtime, it was always so wet, and we had access to the library, to the hall for badminton, and to other rooms for things like chess, stamp club and so on. I went to the Art Room, where I was painting Harriet. I'd asked if I could for my Art continuous assessment.

"Might be a good idea," said old Hamby, grinning. He's a joker, that guy. "Your work's jolly good, Lisa," I started to beam like the Cheshire Cat, "but there isn't enough of it, haha." And he went away chuckling to himself.

"Some people are getting senile," I said. So I painted Harriet. I got to know her face well, but what went on behind it was still a mystery.

Someone who also came to the Art Room was Lindy. And without Karen who was forbidden to go in there because she'd wrecked it on three occasions.

This day we came out together, Harriet, Lindy and me, and Lindy was quite pink and human and chatty. Her leaf and tree prints were really good and she was always better when she was doing something Arty, seemed to have more confidence. Besides, Harriet, though she hardly said anything herself, always got Lindy to chat away merrily.

Karen Arscott sat in the middle of the corridor blocking the way to the classroom. Lindy turned pale, the bruise on her face showing up clearly.

"Whatcher bin doing, then?" said Karen to Lindy.

Without a word Lindy handed over her folder.

"Load o' crap, ain't it?" said Karen and threw Lindy's collection on the floor and stamped on it.

"Any objections?" she went on.

Like a shadow Harriet slipped between her and Lindy, pushed Karen back on to the floor then tipped the chair and Karen up. A bellow of rage echoed down the corridor as Karen lumbered to her feet. A crowd gathered. They were all coming but no one was going to interfere, least of all the boys, though cries of, "Let her have it, Harriet," were heard. Karen charged at Harriet, who waited almost carelessly till the last possible minute, then moved to one side, and Karen crashed heavily into the wall, the picture on the rail above descending on to her head and putting paid to her. A cheer went up. Until,

"Just what is going on here?" said Mr Keithley, the Headmaster.

But Lindy went on her knees beside Karen and lifted her head on to her lap. Harriet, paler than ever, looked at them, then turned and walked through the crowd, who just melted away before her.

I never saw her again.

Mr Keithley, who always seemed to know everything that went on in the school, said Karen had got her deserts at last, and would we please pack up Harriet's things for her as she would be moving on. So we did. Lindy looked after Karen like a mother hen with its chick, and there was no more trouble in that direction. Karen was a changed person. She depended on Lindy a lot.

The weather improved. The sun shone at last. After a time I stopped resenting the dullness of school without Harriet. And, after a longer time, I forgot her and to my surprise found a boyfriend. The portrait? Well, I kept that, though I didn't hand it in for assessment. For one thing it wasn't finished. Besides, I didn't want people looking at it and marking it B or C or lower.

About three years later I went to Art School, and moved my gear into a bedsit for term time. As I was clearing out a drawer, a photo in the old newspaper-lining caught my eye, I don't know why. I looked more closely and saw that it resembled Harriet. But an older Harriet with shorter hair. I realized it was her mother.

Underneath the caption read: Mrs Adrienne Carter was today convicted of the manslaughter of her husband, Frederick Herbert Carter. She attacked and killed him with a heavy stick after he had severely beaten their daughter, Harriet, aged nine years.

Oh, Harriet, Harriet.

Gene Kemp: "I hate potted biographies of me or anyone else, because the story's the thing not the nutter who wrote it. I also hate people asking, 'What do you mean by that on page 43, eh?' I've usually forgotten, and end up saying, 'I've repented now and I'll always wear purple in future,' or something just as useless.

I did write a pot. bio. once, when I was green. It says I have three young children, a three legged gerbil and teach. Well, the children are grown up, the gerbil is dead, bless it, and I no longer stand before a class and yap about their wicked ways. Now I stand in the garden and tell the birds off, instead, because they mess up their bread, and the cheeky things tell me they want some bits of roast instead. Just like school, really.

Ah, I forgot. I do have a hobby. Doing as little as possible for as long as possible."

THE WOODWORK CLASS
Nigel Gray

It was the last week of school before the summer holidays. We were told that we would all be starting to learn woodwork in the autumn and so we went to meet the woodwork teacher, Mr Springer.

Normally nobody wants to do anything during the last week of term. It always feels as if the holiday should have started already. But because, I suppose, this was something new, and different, there wasn't much mucking about. There were all sorts of interesting smells in the woodwork room, like the dusty scent of wood shavings and the pungent stink of glue.

Springy seemed quite nice. "Don't look on woodwork as just another school lesson," he said. "All your lives you'll want to make things with wood. You may want to make a soapbox on wheels this summer holiday. When you're older, and you've got a house, you'll want to put up shelves, or you'll want to mend a bit of furniture when it breaks and you can't afford to replace it with something new. Or you might want to make your kids a rocking horse or a doll's house for a Christmas present."

We were all sitting on stools gathered round at the front of the room. Springy sat on his desk with his hands in his pockets. (Some teachers shouted at you for putting your hands in your pockets, but Springy didn't seem to mind.)

"Normally in this class," he said, "we don't have to sit still. We don't have to sit at desks. We stand up, and move around, and talk to one another. We work at those benches behind you. But, and this is a big but, I won't tolerate any playing around. Anyone who plays the fool goes straight out, and stays out. Because these tools we use in here aren't toys." He took one hand out of his pocket and waved it towards the racks on the wall. "They're real. Used properly, they're absolutely safe. Not used properly, they're lethal. Now, none of your mums and dads want you going home from school with no fingers. So there will be no messing about in this room. Ever! Is that clear?" He glowered round at everybody, but once he'd finished glowering he smiled. "The first thing we have to do, before we start to make anything, is to learn how to use the tools. There's a right way and a wrong way to use every tool. So we might as well make a start today. Now if we want to make something out of wood, what's the first thing we have to do?"

"Buy the wood," Henry called out.

"You're daft, you are," Mary said.

"Well, yes, all right. Buy the wood," said Springy. "Then what?"

"Depends what you're making," said a boy named Donald Davies.

"Well, yes. Obviously." said Springy. He sprang up onto his feet. I noticed that he was wearing trainers like mine. Most of the teachers wear

100

proper shoes. "Let's say we're going to make a bookcase," he said. "What do we do with the wood?"

"Saw it up to the right lengths," said Delroy.

Springy looked down at the floor in front of his feet. "Exactly," he said "Good lad. Well done. So we'll start off by learning to use the saw. You!" he said, pointing straight at me.

My heart started beating faster. I wondered what I'd done, why he was picking on me.

"What's your name?" he said.

"Sara."

"All right, Sara. Go and fetch me a saw. And get a couple of longish pieces of wood from that pile of off-cuts."

I sighed with relief. I wasn't in trouble after all. While I fetched the saw and the wood, Springy walked over to a workbench. He sort of bounced as he walked. I was beginning to realize that there was more to him being called Springy than just his name being Mr Springer.

"Gather round," he said. "Not that close. And stop that pushing! I won't warn you twice!" He glared at the pushers for a moment. Then he looked at me.

"Will these do?" I asked, holding out the wood.

"Yes. Perfect." He took the wood from me and placed one piece in the well of the workbench. He put a square onto the wood and with a pencil he drew a line across. Then shifting the square along about an inch he drew another, and then another, and so on, until there were pencil lines at intervals all the way along the wood. He held his hand out to me for the saw. I gave it to him and he thanked me. "Now," he said. "Stand square to your work. Make sure you clamp the wood firmly with your hand so that it doesn't slide about. Keep your saw, your eye and your arm in line with your cut. You guide the saw with your forefinger. Make the first couple of cuts carefully so you get a little notch in the wood in the right place, then let the saw do the work for you. Apply your pressure on the downstroke. Like so." He sawed through the piece of wood as easily as cutting a cake.

"Right," he said. "Let's have a volunteer. "You," he said, pointing at Donald Davies. Donald took the saw. Then the teacher stood behind him and reached round with both arms. He held one of Donald's hands on the wood and the other on the saw.

"That's the way," he said. "No, no. Pressure on the downstroke." Together they cut through.

"Another volunteer," he said. "You." He pointed to Mary. He helped her in the same way. We each stepped forward in turn. When it was my turn he stood behind me. It was sort of nice having him help you like that. His hands were warm and firm. He helped everybody the same way – till he came to Imran. When Imran took up the saw, Mr Springer stepped back. "OK. Let's see you give it a try," he said. He said it nicely. He was smiling. Imran sawed the wood.

"Keep that shoulder in line with the saw," Springy said. "Good. You're getting the hang of it. That's it. Well done." The little piece of wood fell with a clatter onto the floor. "Next," Springy said.

He went back to putting his arms round every-body then. Till he came to Delroy. Then he stepped back again. "Come on then. Let's see how you get on." Delroy picked up the saw but then he stood stock-still. I thought for a moment he was going to refuse to do it. But then he began sawing. "Good lad," Springy said. "That's the way." He kept his eyes on the saw all the time. "You've got it. Well done."

Afterwards, as we were going out for break, we began talking about Mr Springer.

"Hey, old Springy's not bad," said Donald.

"I think he's lovely," said Mary.

"He's a pig," Delroy said.

"He wasn't too bad," I said.

"You whites are all the same," sneered Delroy.

"Don't be stupid," I said. "What would you think if someone said you blacks are all the same?"

"He couldn't bear to touch me," Delroy said. "Or Imran. Or Johnny Fisher. Why? Because we're black. He's a racist pig!"

"Maybe you were better than us," Mary said. "Maybe you didn't need any help."

"They weren't better than me," said Henry.

"I think he's nice," Mary said. "He's got lovely blue eyes."

"Yeah, he's probably a Nazi," said Delroy.

"All people with blue eyes aren't Nazis," I said.

"My mum says you get a chip on your shoulder and imagine things," Mary said.

"Your mum don't even know me," said Delroy.

"Well, she don't mean you personally. She means you people."

"What does she mean – *you people?*" Delroy snarled.

"Oh, leave it off, Delroy." Mary said. "I think he's nice. And he treats everybody the same."

"Oh yeah!" Delroy said. "He treats everybody the same. Except when he talks to you whites, he looks you in the eyes. And when he talks to one of *us*, he looks down at the floor. Well, next time he does it I'm going to say to him, you might like it better if I *was* down there on the floor, crawling around like some animal. But I ain't there, man!"

"Yeah, but just because *he*'s like that, there's no need to say all whites are the same," I said.

"Oh, shut up, white trash!" he said.

The others wandered off leaving me and Delroy facing each other in the playground up against the school wall.

"Stop being silly," I said. "Suppose you marry a white girl when you grow up – your own children might be white. Are you going to call them white trash?"

"My kids ain't gonna be whities."

"If you've got a white wife, they might be. And even if they're black – they won't call their mother names, will they? They'll be sort of black *and* white."

"Oh, leave off. I ain't gonna get married anyway."

"You're getting so nasty and stupid," I said, "you won't never be able to find anyone who'd have you."

Delroy clenched his fist and looked as though he was about to hit me. Then the tension seemed to go out of him. "Sorry, Sara," he said. "It's not you I'm angry with."

I could see how upset the incident had made him. I remembered how good it had felt to have Springy help me like he had done. And then I felt anger begin to build up in me. "That Springer's a rat-bag," I said. "He's got no right to treat you like that."

"Ah, forget it," Delroy said. "He ain't worth spit."

"It's difficult," I said. "When someone's nice in

some ways, it's hard to realize they can be horrid as well. We like everything to be black and white." I immediately realized what I had said. "Oh, sorry," I added hastily. "I shouldn't have said that." But Delroy just laughed his infectious laugh. And because he was laughing I suddenly plucked up enough courage and blurted out, "There's a disco Friday night. Will you come with me?"

He stopped laughing and looked at me with surprise in those big brown eyes of his. "Yes," he said. "Yes." And he unclenched his fist and took hold of my hand.

Nigel Gray: "I come from Northern Ireland. My wife comes from Sudan. This is a poem I wrote for our son:

You have white skin
and blue eyes.
In South Africa,
where the beaches are white
and the skies blue,
you will be classified
as coloured.

For that reason
be proud
that the brown Nile
from the heart of black Africa
flows through your veins.

When white racists
vomit their abuse
stand up with your black brothers and sisters
to be counted.

When blacks
show symptoms of the same disease
stand up among your white sisters and brothers.

You are a coloured person
with blue eyes,
a black
with white skin,
and you are truly beautiful because
merely by existing
you demonstrate
that love
makes far more sense
than hate."

SEA-COAL
Robert Westall

I was painting me seven-hundredth railing. In wi'
the scraper, ripping off the faded blue flakes, scat-
tering them like flowers on the sick January grass.
Again, I heard the echo of Granda's voice.

"If you're doing owt, son, mek a job of it."

Granda even made a job of dying. Torpedoed
twice in the War, but Jerry couldn't kill him. Fell
off a ladder at the age of seventy-nine, painting his
own guttering. A stroke, the doctor said. Dead
before he hit the ground.

Christ, I miss him.

I eased me muscles, looked back along all the
railings I'd done, stretching down the hill. Glad
they were bright orange, brave against the grey
January sky, the grey works, grey steam billowing
from grey chimneys. Making a lot of steam the
works was, but not much chemical. Hardly a feller
in sight. Rationalisation, they said, redeployment.
Ha bloody ha. That works had been the town's Big
Mammie for a hundred years. Fat pay-packets and
all the copper wire you could nick, smuggled out
wrapped round your belly under your shirt.

Big Mammie's sick, maybe dying. Keep on painting the railings; stops you going bonkers.

Six months back, when we'd just left school and were rotting on the dole, they'd really conned us wi' Job Creation. Moving into the realm of new technology, gaffer said first morning, his spectacles winking shifty under the neon-lights. How to live at peace wi' the computer! Chance of a real job at the end, if you showed the makings!

We really lapped it up, that first morning, in our shining-bright safety-helmets. Overalls so new they argued back as you walked. First lunchtime we swaggered down the shops wearing the lot; clattering our boots 'til we drove the old ganny in the off-licence mad. We are the ICI boys!

Once, I even got a chance to help a fitter wi' a faulty pump. And a fitter is what I want to be. The pump was small, shiny, beautiful piece of craftsmanship. I put my head close to it an' listened, like Granda used to. Which noise was the fault? The thin tapping at the top, or the wheezing like bronchitis in the round, curly middle?

"What yer reckon?" I asked the fitter. That's how fitters talk to each other.

"What yer mean, what yer reckon?" He had a little sneaky putting-down grin on his face.

"What's up wi' pump?"

"Aah don't give two damns. It's coming out, that's all Aah know."

He cut the power wi' a red button; turned a yellow wheel to cut off the flow of chemical. Started undoing the pump's screws. One stuck. He took a hammer to it. The shining metal dented, crumpled, collapsed in a wreck. "Bloody German rubbish," said the fitter, pulling the wrecked pump free and throwing it on a trolley. "Get that packing-case open, kid, will ya? Wi'out breaking what's inside, right?"

Inside was another pump, exactly the same.

"Why didn't we mend the old one?"

"Cheaper to buy new. Pumps is cheaper than fitters."

"Me Granda . . ."

"Your Granda went down wi' the *Titanic*, kid! This is *today*."

"Call yerself a *fitter?*" I shouldn't ha' said it; but he shouldn't ha' said that about Granda. He thought about clouting me one, then noticed me size. He kicked the pump instead, like it was a dead cat, and wheeled it away.

The next week, the pound started climbing against the dollar. The Americans stopped buying chemical. The works started making steam instead. The bosses started walking round like they were going to their own funeral, and we were all put on painting railings . . .

There were eight of us, wi' a foreman, painting the railings round a wood next the works. Within a week, Bowlby began pissing about, snapping the thin branches off the chemically poisoned trees and throwing them in the soupy yellow river. The foreman caught him an' played hell. Bowlby just laughed an' went right on doing it. Soon all the rest were doing it, an' the foreman didn't come round much any more, except wi' the packets on payday.

I tried larkin' about wi' them once; but it made me feel like a little kid, so I jacked it in. There's no point in going backwards. But they went on wi' it. I'd see them through the trees, lighting fires, roasting stolen taties, toasting sandwiches, like chimpanzees in safety-helmets. Sometimes they shouted I was licking foreman's arse, but I ignored them and they soon got tired.

I was halfway down my seven-hundred-an'-first railing when I heard the noise they were making change; their voices went quieter, a creepy sort of gloating. I tried to ignore it, but I knew they were going to hurt something. Something worse than trees. Not me, mind. I'm big, and when I land somebody one. . . .

Finally, I couldn't bear it. I stuck me brush back in the paint and walked towards their sodding fire. One or two of them saw me, and ran ahead through the trees, shouting I was coming.

Bowlby had a cat; a poor thin white thing; from the look on his face, he wasn't thinking of feeding it sandwiches. He had a bit o' rope round its neck. It had its ears back, terrified but still hopeful. It licked his hand.

So it was me an' Bowlby again. It always was. The rest o' the kids were nowt, shadows hanging round the edges.

"What you doing wi' cat?"

"None of your business."

"I'll mek it my business." I looked round the rest. They kept their eyes down. One had a brick in his hand. So they were going to drown the cat. Coulda' been worse. Bowlby'd roast a cat alive. . .

"I'll tek that cat."

Bowlby watched me coming. I began to think that the poor cat was the cheese in the trap; an' I was the poor bloody mouse.

"C'mon, mek me," said Bowlby. I'd have been scared, but for his eyes. They were rovin' all over the place, half cocky, half doubtful. Telegraphing, Granda called it.

I moved in on him. I tell you, I was pig-sick wi' six months o' painting railings. Just lookin' for something to smash that needed smashing. Like Bowlby. But I was scared of hurting the cat . . .

He threw it in my face. A good trick, but for his telegraph-eyes. And I don't play goalie for nowt. I had that poor cat snatched lefthanded against my chest and still had time to see Bowlby's kick coming.

I grabbed his foot and just held it there, giving it the odd twist for good luck. Then I pushed the foot up an' back.

He kept his feet, just. At the cost of running backwards about fifteen feet like something out of Laurel and Hardy. Trouble was it carried him back to the steep, slippery river-bank, and down he went in a slather of foam, like a depth charge exploding in the Yellow Sea.

I laughed myself sick; a shit like Bowlby where he belonged at last. Just in time, I realized nobody else was laughing. Next second, they were all on me. I'd never have thought they had it in them. But they meant it, boots an' all.

I managed. I had to punch one-handed, wi' the cat. But I stood back an' punched big – a couple o' golden handshakes they won't forget. But they just stood back then, an' started throwing things.

I turned me back on them, and walked off through the wood. One stone rattled on me helmet, but they didn't follow. Maybe they were givin' Bowlby the kiss o' life.

I kept walking, blind wi' misery. It wasn't just me bruises; it was suddenly knowing how much they hated me, how they'd planned the whole thing. And the bloody railings, and even that was coming to an end and then it'd be the dole again an' lying in bed 'til children's telly started, trying to think of some reason for getting up. Even school would've been better. And I'd left me flask and sandwiches back there. An' Mam wouldn't let me take the cat home an' the stupid thing would go back to the wood an' the next time they'd do it in for sure. I just hated the whole of bloody 1982 and wished to hell I was somewhere else, anywhere . . .

So I never really grasped how I got out o' the far side o' the wood and into that slum. Never seen a slum like it. They were so poor they couldn't even afford telly; not an aerial in sight. The houses were the usual Coronation Street, but they'd made no efforts, not even a lick o' paint. The streets were cobbles; the gutters full o' dirty soapy water an' little kids were playing in them wi' matchbox-boats, wi' a match for a mast an' a little bit o' paper for a sail. They got up an' stared at me open-mouthed as I walked past. They had big boots an' maroon jerseys that buttoned at the neck an' skin-head haircuts and trousers that hardly covered their knees. Stared at me like I was a Martian, snot hanging from their noses that they wiped on the cuffs o' their jumpers, and great big shadowed eyes. I felt embarrassed, a bit. I suppose I did look funny, walking along wearing a safety-helmet an' carrying a cat. But I hung on to the cat. I had a feeling that if I let go, it wasn't long for this world. It was thin as razor blades, and shivering in great convulsive shivers. Nothing that a month of home-cooking wouldn't cure but . . .

Where was home? I hadn't a clue. Never been down this part of town in me life. The street-name said 'Back Brannen St'. Never heard of it. There were four men on the corner, squatting on their haunches, wearing caps, looking like Norman Wisdom multiplied by four.

"Excuse me," I said, staring down at them.

"Yes, kidder?" asked one, kindly.

"I've got meself a bit lost."

"Ye're a bit big for that. Where'd ye want, kidder?"

"I live on the Marden Estate," I said stiffly.

"Marden Estate? Never heard on it. Hev ye, Jackie?"

Another man shook his head. "Aah've heard of Lord Redescapes' Estate, and Sir Percy Hambly's Estate. Never heard of Marden Estate. Heard of Marden Farm mind – very good place for sheep, is Marden Farm. D'you like roast mutton, kidder?" They all laughed, like there was a private joke they weren't letting on about.

"Marden Farm's near us," I said "except it was demolished 'afore I was born. We still got Marden Farm Road."

"*Demolished?*" asked the first man. "That's a staff-officer's word for ye, Jackie! Last thing Aah saw *demolished* was a German strongpoint in Thiepville Wood." He brought a worn tobacco-tin out of his pocket, and took out a squashed-flat dog-end. With loving care he pressed it back into shape. The tobacco inside rustled dryly. Then he took a pin from his coat-lapel, stuck it through the dog-end and lit up, turning his head carefully sideways, so he didn't burn his nose. He took one drag, and passed it to his mate. I watched as they solemnly passed it round the circle, like an Indian pipe of peace. Holding it by the pin; it had burnt down to quarter of an inch long, too small to hold between their fingers.

"D'you wanna fag?" I burst out, horribly embarrassed. Took twenty king-size from my overalls and flipped it open.

They stared. "Jesus God!" said one. They didn't move. Just stared at the packet of twenty like they'd never seen one before. I grabbed five out of the packet and thrust them into the first man's hand, where it lay on his crouching knees.

He looked at me. "Who are ye, hinny? Carnegie?"

It was all so strange, I ran.

As I turned the corner, I heard their mocking voices, calling like birds.

"Thank you, Carnegie."

But round the corner was worse. A man sat on a doorstep, propped against the door. A fat man with no legs. Instead, he had big round black leather pads where his legs should be; held on by leather straps fastened round his waist. His fat face lifted, as he heard me running. His eyes were covered with small round dark glasses.

"Buy a box of matches, mate?"

I wanted to go on running, but a kind of nosy horror took me up to him. There was a flimsy wooden tray hanging round his neck by a piece of white tape. On it were nine boxes of matches. On the front of the tray was written DISABLED – THREE CHILDREN. There was a greasy cap on the pavement beside him, guarded by an old black dog, nearly as fat as the man.

"Help a wounded soldier, mate!" he said, in a

sing-song voice like a worn gramophone record. "Wife and three kids. Military Medal and bar." He pointed to the breast of his cut-down blue coat. There were four faded medal-ribbons and a silver badge. His whole face strained towards me, through the round black spectacles. "Help an Old Contemptible, mate, what caught it at Wipers!"

I reached desperately into my overalls, and tossed two ten-pence pieces into his cap. His face frowned at the double-clink. He scrabbled for the coins, felt their milled edges; bit them. Then he said,

"Two florins. God bless you, mate." I turned to go, but his big, warm hand reached out and clasped mine. "Don't forget your box of matches, mate. And give us a hand up – it's me dinner-time." Suddenly he had both big hands on my shoulders, and was heaving himself upright onto the black leather pads. I had to brace my free hand against the wall to stop myself being pulled over on top of him. His breath, his warmth, the smell of his overcoat, were like a farm-animal's.

"Thanks, mate." He released me, and reached down for his cap, steadying his tray of matches with a practised hand. How could he be practised at having no legs? How could he exist, and even think of dinner, with no legs?

Unbearable. I ran, the safety-helmet bouncing like a pan on my head, the cat digging its claws into me, clinging on tight.

"You forgot your matches, mate!" I looked back; he was following me, walking slowly on his leather pads, matchbox held aloft.

I ran up a side-alley. And another, and another. I ran a long time. When I came to myself, the alley had turned into a cinder-track between allotments. The allotments had funny high fences, made of the rough bark off pine-trees, cut in weird, wriggly shapes, full of knot-holes. There was a dripping tap, fastened to a wooden post, quite alone on a corner. Dripping gently on the cinders. I suddenly felt very thirsty; my mouth felt like a desert of alkali.

I was still guzzling when I heard a voice say, "You'd better leave a bit of water for the plants." I looked up, dribbling water from my mouth over the cat's fur. Expecting another monster.

But he wasn't a monster. He was a young – bit older than me. Thin, but in a ruddy-faced, fit sort of way. Bright, blue, friendly eyes, and a big ginger moustache, neatly trimmed. The only weird thing about him was his clothes – a battered suit with waistcoat and watch-and-chain. No collar an' tie, only a spotless white muffler. His cap, another Normal Wisdom special, was pushed well back on his ginger curls, and he was leaning over his allotment gate, smoking a pipe. The thin blue smoke curled up in the calm air, and he looked totally contented. It was just funny, him being dressed like some old-age pensioner, and yet looking so young.

"Cat could do wi' a square meal," he said. "Why not give it an Oxo cube?"

"Just rescued it," I said. "Some kids were goin' to drown it."

"Got a few scraps." He opened his gate, as slowly and grandly as if he was the Duke of Newcastle.

Mind you, even the Duke of Newcastle wouldn't have minded owning what was inside. A long path of old brick stretched into the distance, through three trellis archways hung wi' pink roses. The well-raked soil bulged with healthy-looking flowers, better than my dad ever managed; all in well-drilled rows like soldiers on parade. There was a pigeon-cree, painted in green and white stripes, with ornate fretwork on top, full of plump cooing pigeons. Further on, through the third trellis, vegetables. Turnips like cannon balls; cabbages like even bigger cannon balls. Hoed lines of potatoes. A tarred black hut, then a greenhouse full of thin-stemmed tomatoes, with yellow fruit.

My God, all this in January . . . and that explained everything, the hollow-eyed kids, the man with no legs.

I was dreaming.

Now I'm good wi' dreams, 'cos I dream a lot. And I've learnt to control them. If they start turning into a nightmare, I can wake up. But this dream, at the moment, was OK, so I let it be.

"We haven't been introduced," said the moustached guy, suddenly all stiff and formal. "Name's Billy Dack – put it there." He had a grip like a warm six-inch vice.

"Mike Anderton," I said, recovering my hand and flexing it behind my back, to restore the circulation.

He fetched a crumpled packet of greaseproof paper, and began spilling out crusts and white pork-fat on the brick path for the cat. The cat lowered its tail, and ate with a desperate gulping motion.

"No breakfast," said Billy, "like three million others. You in work, then or still at school?

"Job Creation," I said with a grimace, "painting railings."

"You've not starved, though. Ye're a big lad for

your age. Not shavin' yet? Ye look fit enough for a gentleman . . . like to give me a hand?"

He pointed to a five-foot cylinder of rusting iron that stood by the greenhouse. All chimneys and levers and furnace-doors, like a little brother to Stephenson's *Rocket*.

"What the hell is it?" I asked.

He frowned, thunderously. "Watch yer language, son. Or I'll mek ye wash your mouth out wi' soap." His blue eyes were very sharp; he looked like he thought he had the right to wash out my mouth with soap. Ah, well, what did it matter in a dream?

"What is it?" I said, swallowing a sharp crack.

"It's an old donkey-boiler," he said, "off a ship. I'm fitting it into the greenhouse, to keep it warm, come winter."

"I'll give you a hand," I said. We struggled it into the greenhouse, and connected it to the hot-water system somehow, even though the two things clearly weren't meant for each other. He dragged out what he called his box o' bits – lead piping, old brass taps, great hanks of wire, old tin-openers, screws and nuts – a whole packing-case full. I watched him heat bits of metal red-hot in the stove of his hut, and hammer them into shape like a blacksmith.

"Are you a blacksmith?"

"Shipyard-fitter," he said. "'Til they sacked me, the minute Aah finished me apprenticeship. They're building ships wi' apprentices now, they can't afford to employ grown men."

We finished; he packed his box o' bits away. "Each bit o' that could tell its own story," he said. "Never throw owt away, then ye'll never lack for owt. Well, Aah reckon ye've earned a bit o' bait. Kettle's on."

We went back to the hut. My, it was snug. Old black kettle singing on the stove. China cups and saucers wi' little rose-buds on them. Curtains at the window, and even a bunk wi' a patchwork quilt. He saw me looking at the bunk. "Aah sleep here in summer, for a bit o' peace and quiet. There's ten of us in three rooms, back home. Not room to swing a cat."

He looked into the teapot. It was half full of soggy tea-leaves. "Aye, I think that'll stand one more fill." When he poured the tea out, after a lot of stirring, it was as pale as lager; but he spooned two sugars into my cup without asking, and trailed in long strings of condensed milk from a sticky brown tin. It tasted great. Then he took down a tin with Japanese women painted all over it but most of them were worn away. He held it out to me.

It was full of stale, broken cakes. But he looked at me with the grand smile of a king, like he was giving me a real treat, so I took one.

"Aah load the bread carts for a baker every morning. Only takes an hour, and he gives me all yesterday's leftovers. Keeps our family in bread an' cakes all week." He bit with gusto into a vicious-coloured green triangle. My cake tasted like sawdust wi' pink icing, but he was watching, so I ate it.

"Good, eh?" he said. "That's the best cake the baker does. You're a good chooser! And, bye the bye, what ye got yourself apprenticed as a painter for? From the way ye helped me wi' that boiler, ye'd make a canny fitter."

"I want to be a fitter," I spluttered, still battling wi' the sawdust.

"Then why don't you? Paintin's a softy's job. They're signing on apprentices at the North-eastern Marine – all they can lay their hands on. They'll sack ye at twenty-one, like they sacked me. But ye'd have a trade, an' things can't go on being bad forever."

"Me granda served his time at the North-eastern Marine. Goodwin Anderton he was called."

"Aah knew a Goodwin Anderton there," said Billy. "But he was an apprentice wi' me – a lad my age."

We stared at each other in growing silence. There just couldn't be two men called Goodwin Anderton – never in the history of the world. . . .

I took a deep breath and asked shakily, "What's the date, Billy?"

He reached for a pile of newspapers he kept handy for lighting the stove.

"Twenty-third of July – no, that's last Tuesday's – the twenty-sixth of July." The paper he was holding up was the *Daily Mail. But it was twice the size it should be.*

"What year?" I shouted.

"1932, of course."

"Oh, all right," I said to myself. "I'm dreaming and I don't like this dream any more. Wake up." I closed my eyes and willed myself to wake up as usual. All I got was a totally undreamlike pain on my shin. I opened my eyes, to see him grinning and returning the steel-tipped toe of his boot under his chair.

"That wasn't part of no dream, bonnie-lad."

He didn't believe me about 1982 at first. But I had a newspaper, too, tucked into the pocket of me overalls. *The Sun.* He examined it with interest, 'til he got to page three, then he stuffed it straight into the roaring stove.

"Ye mucky-minded little bugger!"

"Everybody reads it where I come from, even me Mam."

"You must have had a bloody funny bringing-up!"

I distracted him with my digital watch-calculator. Only I had a job to stop him taking the back off to see how it worked. I had to distract him again, wi' a king-sized fag. He lit up with gusto, using a burning piece of paper from the stove.

"Big as a toff's cigar!" He inhaled 'til the ends of his ginger moustache twitched.

"A toff like Carnegie?" I asked. He nodded.

"Who is Carnegie?"

"American. Biggest millionaire in the world, son. Lights his cigars wi' hundred-dollar bills." He sounded wistful, as if Carnegie lived in fairyland. And it was that wistfulness that brought it all home to me, that threw me in a panic.

"Billy – I'm caught. If I've travelled in time, how do I get back?"

He eyed me coolly. "Aah believe ye have. Like that feller in H. G. Wells – the Time Traveller. Come to think of it, you do look a bit like something out of H. G. Wells wi' that hat and that cat. Blimey – I'm a poet an' I don't know it!"

"But how do I get back?" I screeched.

"Aah'll bend me mind to it. Mind you, ye've no cause to grumble, even if ye can't get back. Ye've got a grand new pair o' boots there, that I bet don't let in water, and a watch anybody'd give a thousand pounds for, and enough spare flesh on ye to last three months. Come and help me gather sea-coal for the donkey-boiler, while Aah think about your dilemma."

I didn't notice much on our walk down to the sea; I was too worried. But there was a lot of horses and carts about; big piles of manure in every street. And kids running round in bare feet, though Billy said they preferred it that way in summer. I knew a lot of the houses, but there were gaps between, more green fields. And I saw a man with a wooden leg playing an accordion on the street corner.

The beach was just the same. And the castle on the cliffs. And the swimming pool, though it was brand-new concrete then . . .

The beach was cut in half, as if by a knife. The sunny, southern half was full of holidaymakers in deckchairs. A few, men and women, were wearing striped bathing-costumes that covered them nearly as much as clothes. But most people were sitting there in their Sunday best, hats an' all. There were three dignified men, grand wi' moustache and cap and watch-chain, paddling in the water up to their knees, and still looking like they were going to have a chat wi' King George the Vth. Somebody had a wind-up gramophone, and a whole crowd had gathered to listen.

The cold, northern end of the beach, shadowed by the cliffs, was nearly empty. Long black bands ran along it, round the high-tide mark. Sea-coal. Washed out of coal seams in the cliffs, by the waves. Washed off the decks of colliers in storms; washed out of wrecked ships over hundreds of years. I'd run across those black bands as a little lad, grumbled when they'd hurt my feet. Never realized what they were.

People here did. Well away from the holiday-makers, creeping like mice, frightened of being noticed and giving offence, crawled a grey stooping army of old women, thin coughing men and little kids. Each with their soaking black bag.

Between the sea-coalers and the holidaymakers, on the very edge of the sunlight, a policeman was standing, sweating in a serge collar done up to his neck.

"One of the toffs complains," said Billy, "he'll chuck us all off the beach. Aah wish ye'd left that bloody silly helmet behind. Ye're like something out of *The Shape of Things to Come*. Aah suppose Aah should be grateful you've left the bloody cat."

We got down to it. I followed him along one of the curving black bands, picking up the tiny bits of coal. They were mostly smaller than peas. If you found one as big as a cherry, it was an event. You couldn't scoop them up in handfuls, or you just ended up wi' a sackful o' wet sand. You picked 'em one by one, like prize strawberries. If you bent down to pick 'em, your back hurt like hell. If you knelt, you got your knees soaked. I sort of went blind by the end, sweat dripping off me nose, just picking, picking. Billy left me far behind.

I carried me sea-coal home on me back. It dripped and made me bottom wet. We'd just got to the allotment gate when Billy said, "Here's poor Manny Gosling comin'."

A ghost wavered down that cinder-track, a ghost so thin and staring-eyed that I hoped, I prayed, he'd walk straight past. But Billy said kindly, "What fettle the day, Manny?"

The ghost halted, swivelled his head. "Hallo,

123

Marrer. Fair to middlin'." He pulled a spotless white hanky out of his pocket and began to cough into it. The coughing had a life of its own. The coughs grew bigger and bigger. Manny heaved and shook, as if some enormous, invisible animal had landed on his back and was tearing the life out of him. He clung to a fence post with his free hand, and the whole fence shook for twenty yards.

Then the white hanky blossomed a little pink rose. Another. Then a bigger red one. Then a whole bunch of roses. Blood and spit trickled down his spotless white muffler.

"Steady on, Manny," said Billy, gently, putting a strong brown hand over the thin pale hand that clutched the fence. It seemed to help. The coughing got less and less, and finally stopped.

"Better?"

"Better as Aah'll ever be, now."

"Come in for a cup of tea, Marrer." And Billy opened the allotment gate as grandly as he'd opened it for me. But Manny wouldn't go into the hut with us.

"I'll stay out here, Billy. There's more fresh air out here."

"What's up wi' him?" I hissed.

"TB – consumption. He'll never see next spring. First cold east wind'll finish him."

"But *we* can cure TB easy. A few shots of penicillin – piece of cake."

"Aren't *you* the lucky ones?"

"But if I took him back to our time wi' me . . ."

Billy gave me one of his sharp blue looks.

"You're very sure you're going back, all of a sudden. I thowt ye were stuck . . ."

"I've been thinking . . . if I just go back the way I

came . . . it's worth a try."

"Aye, it's that or nowt. Maybe you came on a return ticket, maybe on a single. There's only one way of finding out. But even if ye are on a return ticket, Aah reckon it'll be for one passenger, bonnie-lad, not two."

"Can I try and get Manny through with me?"

"S'up to ye, bonnie-lad. Nowt to do wi' me."

"I'd like you there, in case it doesn't work."

"Aye, well we'll give Manny his tea, and take him an' all. He could do wi' a brave new world, could Manny."

We gave Manny his tea. I thought he was going to start coughing again, over the sawdust-cake, but he managed to swallow it. He also managed to totter as far as Back Brannen St. The legless man was gone, thank God.

At the end of Back Brannen St was a pale blue railing, quite decently painted, with thin-leaved chemically-sick trees behind, that had a familiar look. Billy spoke to a couple of the sunken-eyed kids who were still playing with their matchboxes in the gutter. "Ye seen this feller before?" he said, pointing at me, all cat and and safety-helmet again.

"Yes. He came out of that gate, but we couldn't get in – it's stuck now. It's always stuck."

I pushed the gate. The cat shivered. The gate opened easily. We passed through, all three of us. Trod on through the silent, leafy, July trees. The air grew colder; the sky grew grey. Leaves seemed to be falling; at least the trees got more and more bare. Manny shivered, pulling up his jacket collar round his thin neck.

"Aah cannit go no further, Billy." He sank onto a fallen log. We stood around, awkwardly. Ahead, I was sure I could hear crashings of branches, distant shouts. I thought I saw a glint of firelight through the winter trees; it was coming on dusk.

"*C'mon*, Manny," I said. "You must try. Not much further. There's doctors can make you well over there, Manny. Plenty o' food – nobody goes hungry."

"Sounds like the bleddy kingdom o' heaven," said Manny, and began coughing again.

I looked at Billy; he gave me a straight look back. "I can't walk any further either, son. There's something holding us back." He nodded at the cat, held against my chest. "Reckon that's your return ticket son. I think I seen her over our side 'afore. But she's only a ticket for one . . .'

I knew what he was thinking. If I let Manny hold the cat, Manny would go and I would stay.

"Aah know where Goodwin Anderton lives," said Billy. "He only lives three streets from us. Aah see him nearly every week . . ."

I closed my eyes, and my head swam. Granda. Granda back. Granda young an' strong. A chance to do a real job; build ships instead of painting endless bloody railings. Hitler coming, and the War. Granda survived it, so could I.

I hesitated.

Too long. Manny said, fretful, "Take us home, Billy. Aah'm catching me death o' cold, sitting here."

I looked at Billy again, but he was already hauling Manny to his feet.

"Tara, son," he said, wi'out looking at me. "Aah'll not tell Goodwin ye called – he's a mate o' mine!"

The way he said it, I'd rather he'd hit me.

They didn't seem to be walking very fast, but they vanished quickly amongst the trees, like smoke. At the same moment, the cat jumped out o' me arms and was off. By gum, I was scared then. I ran an' ran, 'til I was right among that lot at the fire.

"What's up wi' you?" asked Bowlby's mate. "You look like you seen a ghost." But Bowlby had knocked off early to get dry, and they weren't in a mood to try anything.

Then, of course, I had to go back; all the way to the gate that led onto Back Brannen St. Just to make sure I hadn't been dreaming after all.

The gate was still there; it needed painting, thick wi' rust. An' it didn't open when I pushed it.

Beyond? A bloody great open space, with drums of chemical piled under black polythene sheets. All the chemical the company couldn't sell to the Americans. Not a sign of Back Brannen St. . . .

It was all fading, just like a dream. I must've dreamed it all, I told meself, walking home.

Except when Mam made me take me dirty boots off, a little piece of coal fell out of them. No bigger than a pea. . .

Robert Westall: "I'm a careers teacher. Every time I walk past those Job Creation boys painting railings, I get a terrible sense of guilt. I talked to my father, who was an apprentice-fitter in the 1920s, and was sacked from the North-eastern Marine the moment he'd finished serving his time. After that, the story wrote itself. Ironically enough, a distant relative of mine is Chairman of British Shipbuilders ..."

FOLLOW ON

The Short Story

What is a short story?

Horror, families, myths, science fiction, sport, neighbours, mystery, travel, school, love, ghosts, Westerns – almost any subject you can think of has been written about in one short story or another. Today the short story is one of the most popular forms of writing used by professional authors, and many are made into plays and films for television and the cinema.

A short story can vary in length from just a few hundred words to as many as 10,000. In this volume 'The Rescue of Karen Arscott' is the shortest at under 1,800 words while 'The Sleeping Beauty of Anton P'ntarr' stretches to over 6,000 words. When asked what is typical about the short story Roald Dahl wrote: "there is no time for the sun shining through the pine trees". What he meant was that the short story writer has to throw the reader right into the action. There is no time to set the scene in the way a full length novel does. With the stories in this book, it is usually the action which is more important than the setting or the characters, though of course all are important.

Talking about short stories

When you are talking about short stories it is useful to know the meaning of certain basic 'technical' words which are used whether you are discussing a short story, a novel or a play.

Plot

The plot refers to the *action* in a story. All of us read through a story because we want to know what happens next and how it will end – rather like the way we wait for a punch-line in a joke! Look at 'Woof' for an example of a tale in which we keep reading because we want to find out just what *will* happen to Wolf Man Kevin.

Characters

These are the *'inhabitants'* of the stories. They may be spirits from the past, lovers from future worlds, young children, teachers or parents. Sometimes characters are described in great detail; at other times, they are only sketched very briefly. And writers often want us to take sides for or against their characters. Think of some examples of *how* characters are written about in these stories.

Setting

This word refers to the *place or period of time* in which the story is set. As with the characters, it is something which the writer can either hint at briefly or describe in great detail. For example, compare the settings and how the authors describe them in 'The Sleeping Beauty of Anton P'ntarr' and 'Sea-Coal'.

Narrator

Of course it is the author – Chrys Bensted, Petronella Breinburg or Jan Dean – who actually writes the words, but all stories are told from a particular *point of view*.

The writer can do one of the following:

1. Pretend to be in the shoes of one of the characters in the story and see everything through that character's eyes. This means that the story will be told using 'I'. And this is called 'first-person narration'.
2. Stand outside the action and look down on it, seeing everything that happens to everyone. Characters are referred to as 'he' or 'she' or 'it'. This is called 'third-person narration'.

Which stories in this collection are told using the 'first-person narrator', and which use the 'third-person narrator'?

Themes

Writers write to tell a story. We read to find out 'what happens next'. But stories often have important *ideas or messages* in them. These are known as themes. Pat Ayinde in 'A Day Too Late' is writing as much about people's prejudices as she is about a visit to an Old People's Home. In 'Sea-Coal' Robert Westall is telling us a great deal about the poverty of the 1930s. What other themes can you find in this collection?

Style

This is something very difficult to define but generally refers to the *way* in which a writer tells the story and brings together characters, plot, setting and theme – in other words, all the ingredients of the story. A ghost story will be told in a different way from a love story or a school story, and all writers have their own habits and tricks of style.

When you are talking about the styles of writers in this book think about some of the following:

- length of sentences and paragraphs. A writer may use longer sentences for detailed descriptions of landscape, but short, sharp sentences when wanting to create tension or suspense.
- attention to detail. For example, look at the description of Sonia's "white satin sheath-dress" in 'School Play'.
- how the writer sets the mood and atmosphere of the tale.
- the opening and closing sentences of a story. Does the writer save up a surprise ending?
- how the writer makes us laugh.
- where the writer wants to focus our attention and who she/ he wants us to take sides with.
- the use of conversations and dialogue.
- the use of language generally; for example, the futuristic words in 'The Sleeping Beauty of Anton P'ntarr'.

131

Writing your own short story

Plan out your own story by asking and answering the following questions:
1. What is going to be the *subject* of the story?
2. Where is it going to take place? Are there going to be several different places?
3. How many characters are there going to be?
4. Are you going to use *first* or *third*-person narration?
5. Are there any particular ideas or themes you want to put across to your reader?
6. Are you going to have lots of dialogue, detailed descriptions, humour, suspense, or what?

Also ask yourself the question: *Who* am I writing for?

A plan for writing
1. Jot down your ideas for the story.
2. Sort out roughly how many paragraphs you'll need. How long will the story be?
3. Write out your story in rough.
4. Ask somebody to read it through with you. How would they make it better?
5. Rewrite the story, paying careful attention to spelling, sentences and paragraphs.
6. Read it over once more to see that you haven't made any silly mistakes or basic errors.

Getting started
In an essay titled 'Lucky Break' Roald Dahl describes how he first became a writer. These are some words of advice from him.

Here are some of the qualities you should possess or should try to acquire if you wish to become a fiction writer:
1. You should have a lively imagination.
2. You should be able to write well. By that I mean you should be able to make a scene come alive in the reader's mind. Not everybody has this ability. It is a gift, and you either have it or you don't.

132

3. You must have stamina. In other words, you must be able to stick to what you are doing and never give up, for hour after hour, day after day, week after week and month after month.
4. You must be a perfectionist. That means you must never be satisfied with what you have written until you have re-written it again and again, making it as good as you possibly can.
5. You must have strong self-discipline. You are working alone. No one is employing you. No one is around to give you the sack if you don't turn up for work, or to tick you off if you start slacking.
6. It helps a lot if you have a keen sense of humour. This is not essential when writing for grown-ups, but for children, it's vital.
7. You must have a degree of humility. The writer who thinks that his work is marvellous is heading for trouble.

Roald Dahl

GOOD LUCK WITH YOUR WRITING!

Do You Read Me?

Points for discussion
1. How are we shown that Rodney has "difficulty in communicating"?
2. How does he make up for this?
3. How many different slogan-badges are mentioned in the story?
4. What reasons does Mr Fenton give to Rodney for reducing the number of badges he wears?
5. Why does Rodney feel "like Gulliver in Lilliput" at the Book Fair?
6. What view does Rodney have of himself?
7. What do "the visual cream of his class" think of him?
8. What does the last line of the story suggest about Rodney and Liz?

Further activities

- Make a list of all the words and phrases in the story which tell you something about Rodney. Now write a short description of him as if he were 'coming through the door now'. How would he be treated if he were in your class all the time?

- Use one of the following 'slogans' as a starting point for your own short story or play:
  WATCH THIS SPACE
  NO FLIES ON ROD
  READ THE SMALL PRINT
  IF YOU CAN READ THIS YOU ARE TOO CLOSE

- Rewrite 'Do You Read Me?' imagining that Rodney is telling it from *his* point of view. Study the story carefully to see what changes you will have to make.

- One of the issues raised in this story is whether pupils should be allowed to wear badges at school. Hold a debate – as a class or in groups – with the motion: 'This House believes all badges should be banned in schools'.

Further reading

Jan Mark has written many tales for and about young people. Two particularly enjoyable collections of her short stories are *Nothing to be Afraid Of* and *Hairs in the Palm of the Hand*. You can find the story 'The Choice is Yours' in *Round Two*. Her novels include *Thunder and Lightnings* and *Under the Autumn Garden*. Her play *Izzy* about a West Indian girl who, like Rodney, is a bit of a loner, is ideal for class or group reading.

Woof

Points for discussion

1. Why is the story titled 'Woof'? Can you think of a better one?

2. "Kevin had won". In what way does Kevin 'win' in his meeting with Mr Tanner and Mr Southall?

3. Which sentence in the story *first* suggests there is going to be conflict between Mr Crockett and Kevin? Look carefully at the text.

4. How does the Head deal with Kevin when he interviews him?
5. "They thought it was just a game ... but they were wrong" (page 19). What do you understand by this phrase? Do you feel it *is* all a game for Kevin?
6. Which sentence tells us that Kevin is infamous throughout the school?
7. What is Jack Crockett's opinion of the Third Years? How does he treat them?
8. Why do you think Crockett behaves towards Kevin the way he does? Do you find the scene in the Metalwork Room realistic or not?
9. We guess that Kevin is responsible for the gas explosion. Do you think he is justified in causing the "spate of accidents"?
10. What do you understand by the last few lines of the story?

Further activities
- Imagine you are one of Kevin's teachers. Improvise a couple of scenes with him:
     (i) in which you have a row in the classroom
     (ii) in which you talk alone with Kevin about his behaviour.
- Jan Dean writes in her note that the story tries "to say something about tensions in schools" (page 25). Write your own short story or play about a time when tensions occurred in your own school or classroom.
- Look up the poem 'Dumb Insolence' by Adrian Mitchell (in *Strictly Private*). It is all about tensions between pupils and teachers – and how pupils can skilfully get the upper hand. It begins:

     I'm big for ten years old
     Maybe that's why they get at me

     Teachers, parents, cops
     Always getting at me

     When they get at me

     I don't hit 'em
     They can do you for that

Write your own poems on this subject.
- Look back to page 24: "Jack Crockett turned to the class. He had made his point". Now write your own ending to the story to follow these words. This could be done as narrative or as a play with two or three scenes in it.
- Here is a report slip for Kevin's school:

Mayfield School

Subject ....

Ability .... ,

Effort ....

Comment:

                                              Teacher ....

Complete reports for several of the subjects Kevin takes, including ones written by his form tutor and headmaster.

Further reading
There are many stories and novels about school-life, often with characters rather like Kevin. If you don't already know them, try the novels of Robert Leeson: *The Third Class Genie* and the *Grange Hill* books. *The Chocolate War* by Robert Cormier, *The Goalkeeper's Revenge* by Bill Naughton, *Summer's End* by Archie Hill, *Cider With Rosie* by Laurie Lee and George Layton's *The Fib and other stories* – all have lively accounts of classroom events.

School Play

Points for discussion

1. What does Amanda Barnes mean when she says about the play that she had "the doubtful privilege of getting it all together"?
2. Why does Amanda choose Andy for the part of Prince Charming and Sonia for Cinderella?
3. Why does Sonia claim to be seeing Mr Winters out of school?
4. How does Sonia react to the news that Mr Winters is to be the stand-in Prince Charming? And why?
5. Why does Sonia dress up in the way she does?
6. "How *dare* he. How *dare* he look at me like that!" (page 33). Why does Sonia behave in this way after the play has finished?
7. "So what was the next role for Sonia – Hell's Angel?" (page 34). What does this comment suggest about Sonia's character?

Further activities

- Imagine Sonia keeps a diary. Write her entries for the weeks covering the rehearsals and performance of the play.
- Write your own short story or play about a school production in which *everything* goes wrong. Make it as funny as you can. Act out your play.
- Draw a strip-cartoon of the story. Plan by making a list of about nine or ten interesting 'snapshots' of the story.
- Hold a post-mortem on 'School Play'. In groups, each person has to choose one of the characters in the story and then discuss the part they have played. Sonia might have to justify why she dressed up; Mr Winters has to explain his staring at Sonia, etc.
- You are a reporter on the local evening newspaper. Write a short report on the school production. Give it an eye-catching headline!

Further reading

There are a number of entertaining plays which have school

settings. You might like to sample the following: the *Grange Hill* plays; *Gregory's Girl*, adapted from the film of the same name; *Closed Circuit*, a futuristic play in which the entire education system is computer based and teachers have become obsolete.

A Day Too Late

Points for discussion
1. Why do the girls visit the Old People's Home?
2. What does Mrs Clarke feel is the most important thing about the girls coming to the Home?
3. What impressions do the girls form on their first visit?
4. Why does Sarah hope to "get a talkative one" (page 39)?
5. What does Sarah learn about Mrs Miles's family?
6. "Sarah could not think which bit of history, geography, ethics or economics would most enlighten Mrs Miles" (page 41). What does Sarah mean by this?
7. "It is part of the experience to learn how to cope with other people's nastiness" (page 36). What does Sarah learn from her meeting with Mrs Miles?
8. What are Mrs Miles's thoughts after the girls have left?
9. What are your feelings at the end of the story?

Further activities
- How would you have reacted in Sarah's position? Do you agree with Yvette's comments on page 43? Improvise a conversation you have with Mrs Miles the next day in which you talk about people's prejudices.
- Use one of the following titles as a starting point for a short play or piece of improvisation:
  Mistaken Identity
  An Hour Too Late
  The Apology
  The Old Folks' Home
  Pride and Prejudice
- Pat Ayinde writes: "So often we are prejudiced by first impressions of what a person is wearing, how they look, or what colour their skin is" (page 47). Write a short story – real or imaginary – on this subject.

- Improvise a scene in which two people meet, take an instant dislike to each other, but then gradually become more friendly. Tape the scene, then write it up as a play.
- Have you been involved in any community work or neighbourhood projects? If you have, prepare a talk for the class/group on what this involved.

Further reading
The subject of prejudice – particularly racial prejudice – is at the heart of many poems, plays and novels. You might like to read some of the following: 'Telephone Conversation', a poem by Wole Soyinka; Farrukh Dhondy's collections of short stories *East End at Your Feet* and *Come to Mecca*; *Walkabout* by James Vance Marshall; *To Kill a Mockingbird* by Harper Lee; *Roll of Thunder, Hear my Cry* by Mildred Taylor; *Black Like Me* by John Griffin; and the short story 'Jamaican Fragment' by A. Hendricks in *City Stories*.

(See also *Further reading* under 'The Woodwork Class')

The Sleeping Beauty of Anton P'ntarr

Points for discussion
1. Why does the author begin with his note about Hoth's Crib? Would the story itself be successful without this introduction?
2. Why is the girl, Mede, working at the Inner-Space Menagerie?
3. "You shouldn't overlook the cultural persistence of the white smile" (page 51). What does Anton mean by this? Think about advertisements on television!
4. What phrase does Mede use to suggest that Anton 'has a screw loose'?
5. Why does Anton's mother warn her children not to refer to the Troglodyte Dwellings as 'caves'?
6. Why does Anton not want to go on "a time sleep" with the rest of the family?

7. How does school registration take place in this future world?
8. Why is the mythological Hoth carved on the door of the Institute of Longevity?
9. Why do you think the family receive "anti-dream injections" before they Travel On?
10. What happens to Anton at the end of the story?

Further activities

- What other myths or legends about the Gods and Death have you read? Compile a little booklet on this topic, include some drawings.
- Make a list of all the 'science-fiction' ingredients in the story. Then list all the 'love-story' ingredients. Are they ones that you expect to find in these kinds of stories? And what does the title lead us to expect?
- Imagine that this story is the first chapter of a novel. Write the next chapter, perhaps including a map of the journey Anton or his family make. Design an eye-catching cover for the book.
- Would you accept the invitation to 'Travel On' for 200 years, 150 years, or for 99 years and a day? Write a short story or play based on this idea.
- Imagine yourself landing in a future world. Improvise a scene in which you meet aliens from this other planet.

Further reading

Science-fiction is a very popular subject with writers. The following anthologies contain some excellent material for young readers: *Science Fiction* edited by James Gibson (John Murray); *Science Fiction* edited by John Foster (Ward Lock); *13 Science Fiction Stories* by Paul Groves and Nigel Grimshaw. Ray Bradbury, Isaac Asimov and Arthur C. Clarke are names worth looking out for in the science-fiction genre. The novels of Nicholas Fisk and Douglas Hill are also recommended.

Suddenly There Came a Crack in the Ice

Points for discussion

1. Why were the girls and boys told by teachers to remove their hats?
2. What sacred rule does Cita break at the start of the story? Why does she do this?
3. What causes the friendship between Teneke and Cita to break up?
4. What are Cita's views about speaking her own language in school?
5. What advice does Johan give her?
6. How do Teneke and the other girls plan to help Cita?
7. What are Cita's feelings and thoughts as the story ends?
8. Why do you think this particular rule about language existed in her school?
9. In what ways does the title link to the various scenes and ideas in the story?

Further activities

- Are there pupils in your class who speak and write English at school and another language at home? What problems and advantages do they find? If you are lucky enough to be bilingual, talk to your class/group about the advantages this gives you.
- Carry out a survey in your class or year group to see how many different languages are spoken by pupils. Draw up a chart to summarise your findings. Put together a collage of writing in the various languages you have come across.
- Put yourself in Cita's position. Act out a scene in which you discuss the language issue with a teacher. Then write a letter to the local newspaper stating your arguments about speaking Surinams.
- Improvise some scenes in which a group of people meet and try to make themselves understood even though they all speak different languages.
- Write your own short story or play using one of the following titles:

Rules, Rules, Rules!
Suspended
The Petition
The Ice is Cracking

Further reading
An interesting novel about a boy with a particular language problem is *The Trouble With Donovan Croft* by Bernard Ashley. If you want to read first-hand accounts from young people about their impressions on moving to a new country and culture, the following are recommended: *Our lives* (ILEA English Centre); *Finding A Voice*, edited by Amrit Wilson; *Sumitra's Story* by Rubshana Smith; *Poona Company* by Farrukh Dhondy. Petronella Breinburg herself writes often about multi-ethnic and multi-lingual settings. You might like to read her novel *Us Boys of Westcroft*.

Flying Dustbins

Points for discussion
1. What tells us in the opening paragraphs that the story is set in wartime?
2. What other details in the story reinforce the wartime setting?
3. What picture do you have of Miss Lindley from the opening scenes? Do you sympathise with her?
4. What do we learn about Simon from the same scenes?
5. What does the title of the story refer to?
6. Why is Juliet pleased to hear that Miss Lindley has not been sacked from teaching?
7. What changes the children's attitudes to Miss Lindley?
8. Why, at the end, have Simon's classmates stopped bullying him?

Further activities
• After reading this story involving classroom chaos, look out the poem 'The Lesson' by Roger McGough in *You Tell Me*. It begins:

Chaos ruled OK in the classroom
as bravely the teacher walked in
the hooligans ignored him
his voice was lost in the din

'The theme for today is violence
and homework will be set
I'm going to teach you a lesson
one that you'll never forget'

Write your own poem with this title. Include some real examples from your lessons.

- Use one of the following titles for a short story:
D-Day!
The Secret Weapon
Bullying
'She must have got the sack ...'

- Write a couple of paragraphs – which could be added to the story on page 84 after the words "She must have got the sack" – describing Miss Lindley's thoughts and feelings when she arrives home at the end of the school-day.

- Using the details in 'Flying Dustbins' to start you off, put together a project on life for civilians during the Second World War in England. Look up some historical background in the library. Collect any wartime bric-a-brac you can find – eg. medals, flags, identity discs, newspaper cuttings, photographs, etc. Tape record interviews with anyone you know who lived through the war. Mount the project as a display in your classroom.

Further reading

David Rees has also written a splendid and very exciting novel set in the Second World War called *The Exeter Blitz*. Two other novels with a similar setting are *The Machine Gunners* by Robert Westall and *Fireweed* by Jill Paton Walsh. *Conrad's War* by Andrew Davies offers an 'alternative' view of war. David Rees's other books for young readers include *The Green Bough of Liberty*, *The Missing German* and *The Lighthouse*.

The Rescue of Karen Arscott

Points for discussion

1. "Amongst us lot she stuck out like a sore thumb. Or rather an orchid on a rubbish tip" (page 92). What ideas does this start us thinking about right at the beginning of the story?
2. What do we learn about the narrator in the course of the tale?
3. What picture do you form of Karen?
4. How does the writer create a sense of mystery around Harriet? What do her classmates think of her?
5. Why do you think Karen changes after the incident with Harriet?
6. Why does the narrator not hand in her portrait of Harriet for assessment?
7. What do the last few lines add to the story? Do they explain Harriet's character and actions?
8. Why do you think Gene Kemp titled the story 'The *Rescue* of Karen Arscott'?

Further activities

- You are the narrator of the story. Imagine you meet up with Harriet while at Art School. Act out a scene in which you both look back to the time you were at school together; in particular to the incident with Karen.
- Imagine you are Harriet. Rewrite 'The Rescue of Karen Arscott' in the form of a series of diary entries that you made at the time.
- "Rumours ran round the school that (a) she was a South American millionairess in hiding because of kidnapping threats, (b) she was a refugee from Eastern Europe" (page 94). Take one of these rumours as being the truth about Harriet and write the story of how she came to arrive at the school.
- Bullying is a fact of school life. Talk about the ways pupils and teachers can deal with bullies.
  Improvise a scene in which a class bully is taught a lesson, verbally rather than physically.

Further reading

Two other stories centring on 'bullies' are 'Millicent' by Merle Hodge in *Over Our Way* and 'The Third Thing' by W. Chalk in *The Talking Machine*.

Gene Kemp is well-known as a children's author. Her short stories 'May Queen' and 'Joe's Cat' are available in *Round Two*. She has also written a collection of stories about animals and children *Dog Days and Cat Naps*, and two lively, action-packed novels about forceful youngsters *The Turbulent Term of Tyke Tiler* and *Gowie Corby Plays Chicken*.

The Woodwork Class

Points for discussion

1. Why are the pupils interested in the woodwork room? In what ways is the subject made to seem relevant to them?
2. How does Mr Springer establish discipline in the workshop?
3. In what ways is Springy different from the other teachers? Why do most of the pupils enjoy his lesson?
4. Do you think the teacher is aware of treating Delroy and Imran differently?
5. What causes the tension to go out of Delroy?
6. Do you agree with Sara's words that "We like everything to be black and white" (page 105)?
7. What ideas are common to both the story and the poem (page 106) that Nigel Gray wrote for his son?

Further activities

- The subject of racial prejudice has always been a difficult one in society. Hold a class/group discussion on what part schools should play in trying to improve race relations.
- Improvise a scene in which all the pupils mentioned in the story meet later to talk about Mr Springer's actions.
- Write your own short story or play on the theme of race relations or racial prejudice. Try to create a plot in which some lessons are learned by the characters, as in 'The Woodwork Class'.
- Rewrite the story as a play for radio. Begin by sorting out all the lines actually *spoken*; decide on the number of

scenes; you will also need sound effects and perhaps some
music for an introduction and ending. Set the script out
carefully on the page, with characters' names in a left-
hand margin. Tape a group reading of your finished play.

Further reading
'Jeffie Lemmington and Me' by Merle Hodge (in *Round Two*)
is an engaging tale with a similar theme to 'The Woodwork
Class'. Novels which have a sensitive treatment of racial
issues include: *The Cay* by Theodore Taylor, *Basketball Game*
by Julius Lester, *Playing It Right* by Tony Drake, and *My
Mate Shofiq* by Jan Needle. Richard Wright's *Black Boy* is
recommended for older readers.

(See also *Further reading* under 'A Day Too Late')

Sea-Coal

Points for discussion
1. What sort of 'writing mood' is the author in, judging by
   the opening couple of pages and by his note on page 128?
2. What are the narrator's feelings towards his Granda?
3. "That works had been the town's Big Mammie for a
   hundred years" (page 107). Explain what this means.
4. Why does the narrator feel conned by the Job Creation
   scheme?
5. What sort of a character is Bowlby?
6. Look back over the story – carefully! At what point did
   you *first* realise that the narrator had travelled back in
   time?
7. At what point does the narrator realise he has been
   dreaming?
8. What feature does the narrator find most striking about
   the beach fifty years back?
9. What effect does the writer want to create by ending the
   story in the way he does?
10. Robert Westall is a Careers teacher; do you think he is
    trying to draw some parallels between young people
    today and in 1932? What might these be?

Further activities

- Make a list of all the things about life in the 1930s that are referred to in the story. Then do your own library research to add to your picture of this period in England. Put together a short project on 'The Thirties'.

- Imagine you are making a television play based on this story. First, make an outline plan of the different scenes you'll want to include. Then draft the script, with directions for actors/actresses and the camera-crew. Edit and redraft the script. Write it up neatly. Act out the play with your group.

- Imagine that the narrator of the story claims that his adventures were not a dream but a *real* step back in time. You are a local reporter. Interview the narrator and then write a feature article on the subject for your newspaper. Think up an exciting headline.

- Choose a period of history that interests you. Do some research. Make notes from your reading. Now write a short story set near your home during the period you have chosen. It could be the year 1900, or even 1066! But remember to include only true historical details, as Robert Westall does in 'Sea-Coal'.

Further reading

Robert Westall has written many excellent novels for young readers. *The Machine Gunners* is an exciting story with plenty of wartime historical detail, while *The Devil on the Road* takes readers back to the time of the Witchfinders.

You might also like to read the following, all of which are novels with strong historical backgrounds and settings: *The Slave Dancer* by Paula Fox; *Friedrich* by Hans Peter Richter; *The Upstairs Room* by Johanna Reiss; *The Milldale Riot* by Freda Nichols; *A Question of Courage* by Marjorie Darke; *Song For a Dark Queen* by Rosemary Sutcliff; *Smith* by Leon Garfield.

Ideas for group and individual work

- All the stories in this collection offer some kind of picture of school life – either past, present or future. What common ingredients do they share? What do you think makes for a successful 'school story'? Write your own School Story, real or imaginary.
- Which characters did you like or identify with? Write your own story about one of these characters. Or bring together characters from different stories – what about a story with Wolf Man Kevin from 'Woof' and Mr Springer from 'The Woodwork Class'?
- What are your reactions to the ways the stories end? If you don't like one of the endings, try rewriting or acting out a different one.
- Take the last lines of any of the stories and write some scenes that might follow on. Act them out in groups.
- Look back carefully over the stories. In each story you will be able to find a place – perhaps soon after the start or half-way through – where the story takes a certain turn in direction. It moves in one way rather than another. Start from one of these moments and rewrite the rest of the story in a different way.
- Some of the authors have tried to bring out the humour and fun of events and characters in their stories. Look back over them and talk about where and how they have succeeded in doing this. 'Do You Read Me?' is perhaps the best story to begin with.
- Chrys Bensted in 'School Play' uses first-person 'I' narration, while in 'Suddenly There Came a Crack in the Ice' Petronella Breinburg has a third-person narrator observing the action from outside. Which type of narrator is used in each of the ten stories?

  What seem to you the advantages and disadvantages of the different types? Rewrite one of the stories, changing the narrator. For example, you could retell 'Flying Dustbins' from Miss Lindley's point of view.

148

- As well as telling a story writers often want to make us think carefully about an idea or a theme.

  What ideas or themes have you come across in these stories?

  Have any of the stories made you think about a subject – like bullying or racial prejudice – which you have not thought about before?

  Have they changed your opinions about anything?

- When we write a story we often base it on something we have seen or done ourselves. If someone writes a book about himself or herself it's called an autobiography. Think about these stories and about what the authors themselves have written in their notes. Do you think any of the stories are partly or completely autobiographical?

- All of the stories are about relationships – usually those between pupils and teachers. From your own experiences of school, do they seem realistic? Which of them *could* have happened in your school?

- Put together your own short story anthology. Begin by including a retelling of one of the stories in *School's O.K.* You might like to make your collection all about school – or include five or six stories of different types: ones about sport or ghosts or a Whodunnit?

  Design an eye-catching cover for your anthology. The school library might like your finished book to put on the shelves for other pupils to read.

- Why does someone behave in the way they do? What causes them to take one line of action rather than another? What motivates the characters in these stories?

  Working in groups, choose one of the stories. Then take it in turns to play the part of one of the characters. Each character is placed in the witness-box and quizzed by the others as to why they behaved as they did in the story. You might start with 'The Rescue of Karen Arscott' or 'Woof'.

- Improvise a 'phone-in' with any of the authors in this volume. One person takes the part of the author. Other members of the group put questions to her/him about plot, characters and themes in the story. Tape record your conversations.

- Mount a dramatised reading – complete with sound effects and music – of one of the stories. This is best practised in groups and then performed to the rest of the class. Prepare a printed programme (with illustrations) for your audience.

Write a review

Which of the stories did you enjoy most? Write a short review of your favourite story from this collection which will make other people want to read it. The plan below offers some starting points.

Writing a review
Setting
Where is the story set?
When are the events taking place?
Is there a special mood or atmosphere to the story?

Plot
How does the story begin?
What is the story about?
Are the events ordinary and everyday – or *extra*ordinary?
Do the scenes follow on from one another – or is there a flashback?
Where are the climaxes?
How does the story end? With a twist in the tale?

Characters
Who are the main characters?
What are they like? Sex, age, nationality, etc.?
Do you find them interesting?
Do you take sides with any of them?
Do they face a problem? Do they solve it?

Style
Who is telling the story? First or third-person narrator?
Are there any special effects used?
How is dialogue used?
Are there lots of long descriptions?
Is there humour or suspense?

Themes
Why do you think the writer wrote the story?
Are there any special messages or ideas?

General
Did you learn anything from the story?
Did you enjoy it?
Will you look for other stories by the same writer? Why?
Would you recommend it to your friends?

(Note: Not *all* of these questions are useful *all* of the time!)

Further reading

Note: Where a book is published in both hardback and paperback editions, details of paperback only are given.

Do You Read Me?

Jan Mark, short stories – 'The Choice is Yours' in *Round Two*, Unwin Hyman Short Stories, Unwin Hyman, 1985; *Nothing to be Afraid of*, Puffin, 1982; *Hairs in the Palm of the Hand*, Kestrel, 1981; novels – *Thunder and Lightnings*, Puffin, 1978; *Under The Autumn Garden*, Puffin, 1980; plays – *Izzy*, Star Plays, Longman, 1985

Woof

Robert Leeson, *The Third Class Genie*, Armada, 1975; *Grange Hill Goes Wild*, Armada, 1980; *Grange Hill for Sale*, Armada, 1981;
Robert Cormier, *The Chocolate War*, Macmillan, 1978;
Bill Naughton, *The Goalkeeper's Revenge and Other Stories*, New Windmill Series, Heinemann Educational Books, 1967;
Archie Hill, *Summer's End*, Wheaton, 1979;
Laurie Lee, *Cider With Rosie*, Penguin, 1970;
George Layton, *The Fib and Other Stories*, Fontana Lions, 1981;
Roger McGough, *Strictly Private*, Puffin, 1982

School Play

Grange Hill 1 and *Grange Hill 2*, Star Plays series, Longman, 1985; *Gregory's Girl* and *Closed Circuit*, Act Now series, Cambridge University Press, 1983.

A Day Too Late

Wole Soyinka, 'Telephone Conversation' in *The Experience of Colour*, Longman Imprint, 1979;
Farrukh Dhondy, *East End at Your Feet*, Macmillan Topliner, 1976; *Come To Mecca and Other Stories*, Armada, 1978;
James Vance Marshall, *Walkabout*, Puffin, 1980;
Harper Lee, *To Kill a Mockingbird*, Pan, 1974;
Mildred Taylor, *Roll of Thunder, Hear My Cry*, Puffin, 1980;
John Griffin, *Black Like Me*, Panther, 1969;
A. Hendricks, 'Jamaican Fragment' in *City Stories*, Ward Lock Educational, 1979

The Sleeping Beauty of Anton P'ntarr

James Gibson, ed., *Science Fiction*, John Murray, 1978;
John L. Foster, ed., *Science Fiction*, Ward Lock, 1975;
Paul Groves and Nigel Grimshaw, *13 Science Fiction Stories*, Edward Arnold, 1979;
Nicholas Fisk, *On the Flip Side*, Kestrel, 1983; *Antigrav*, Puffin, 1982;
Douglas Hill, *Galactic Warlord*, Piccolo, 1980

Suddenly There Came a Crack in the Ice

Petronella Breinburg, *Us Boys of Westcroft*, Macmillan Topliner, 1975;
Bernard Ashley, *The Trouble with Donovan Croft*, Puffin, 1977;
Our Lives, ILEA English Centre, 1979;
Amrit Wilson, ed., *Finding a Voice: Asian Women in Britain*, Virago, 1978;
Rukshana Smith, *Sumitra's Story*, Bodley Head, 1982;
Farrukh Dhondy, *Poona Company*, Gollancz, 1980

Flying Dustbins

David Rees, *The Exeter Blitz*, New Windmill Series, Heinemann Educational Books, 1981; *The Green Bough of Liberty*, Dobson, 1980; *The Missing German*, Dobson, 1977; *The Lighthouse*, Dobson, 1980.
Robert Westall, *The Machine Gunners*, Puffin, 1977;
Jill Paton Walsh, *Fireweed*, Puffin, 1972;
Andrew Davies, *Conrad's War*, New Windmill Series, Heinemann Educational Books, 1981;
Roger McGough and Michael Rosen, *You Tell Me*, Puffin, 1981

The Rescue of Karen Arscott

Gene Kemp, short stories – 'May Queen' and 'Joe's Cat' in *Round Two*, Unwin Hyman Short Stories, Unwin Hyman, 1985; *Dog Days and Cat Naps*, Puffin, 1983; novels – *The Turbulent Term of Tyke Tiler*, Puffin, 1979; *Gowie Corby Plays Chicken*, Puffin 1979;
Merle Hodge, 'Millicent' in *Over Our Way*, edited by Jean D'Costa and Velma Pollard, Longman Caribbean, 1980;
W. Chalk, 'The Third Thing' in *The Talking Machine*, Heinemann Educational Books, 1967

The Woodwork Class

Merle Hodge, 'Jeffie Lemmington and Me' in *Round Two*, Unwin Hyman Short Stories, Unwin Hyman, 1985;
Theodore Taylor, *The Cay*, Puffin, 1973;
Julius Lester, *Basketball Game*, Puffin, 1977;
Tony Drake, *Playing It Right*, Puffin, 1981;
Jan Needle, *My Mate Shofiq*, Fontana Lions, 1979;
Richard Wright, *Black Boy*, Longman Imprint, 1970

Sea-Coal

Robert Westall, *The Machine Gunners*, Macmillan Educational, 1980; *The Devil on the Road*, Puffin, 1981;
Paula Fox, *The Slave Dancer*, Macmillan Educational, 1979;
Hans Peter Richter, *Friedrich*, New Windmill Series, Heinemann Educational Books, 1978;

Johanna Reiss, *The Upstairs Room*, Puffin, 1979;
Freda Nichols, *The Milldale Riot*, Ginn, 1965;
Marjorie Darke, A Question of Courage, Armada, 1978;
Rosemary Sutcliff, *Song for a Dark Queen*, Knight Books,
Hodder and Stoughton, 1980;
Leon Garfield, *Smith*, Puffin, 1970